SIGNS OF THE APOSTLES

SIGNS OF THE APOSTLES

Observations on Pentecostalism Old and
New

WALTER J. CHANTRY

THE BANNER OF TRUTH TRUST

THE BANNER OF TRUTH TRUST
The Grey House, 3 Murrayfield Road, Edinburgh
EH12 6EL
PO Box 621, Carlisle, Pennsylvania 17013, USA

*

© *Walter J. Chantry* 1973
First published 1973
Second Edition, revised, 1976
ISBN 0 85151 175 9

*

*Printed and bound in Great Britain
by Hazell Watson & Viney Ltd,
Aylesbury, Bucks*

Contents

Foreword to the Second Edition   vii

1. REPORTS OF SIGNS AND WONDERS   1

2. STATING THE QUESTION PRECISELY   6

3. MIRACLE-WORKERS SENT FROM GOD 10
   Old Testament Miracles   10
   Messianic Miracles   14
   Apostolic Miracles   17

4. IS SCRIPTURE COMPLETE?   22
   A Pertinent Question   22
   An Evident Answer   29

5. GIFTS IN THE EARLY CHURCH   38
   A Warning   41
   General Principles about Gifts   44
   Gifts No Sign of Grace   45
   Love in Exercising Gifts   48
   Gifts must Depart from the Church   49
   Supervision of Temporary Gifts   54
   One Purpose for Tongues   57

6. WHY CHRISTIANS SEEK 'THE GIFTS'   61
   Today's Appeal   61
   Corinthian Appeal   68
   Biblical Response   71

Contents

7. BAPTISM WITH THE SPIRIT   82

8. WHEN THE SPIRIT COMES   96
   The Spirit of Holiness   97
   The Spirit of Truth   105

9. PERPLEXING EXPERIENCE   116

10. A POSITIVE WORD   120

11. THE HOLY SPIRIT AND REVIVALS   128

Appendix   140

Select Bibliography   147

Foreword to the Second Edition

Some who read these pages will have read the first edition of 1973. To them certain changes will, I hope, be evident. Putting one's views into print is a humbling business. It invites response and criticism. Most painful, yet most helpful to both mind and soul, is the deserved rebuke of friends. This second attempt to speak to an urgent issue of the times will reflect a twofold reaction to honest suggestions and criticisms.

First, I have aimed at correcting unjust generalizations regarding Pentecostal brethren in Christ. I must apologize for harsh remarks in the last volume which fell with unwarranted universal application. If I have not now succeeded, I have at least laboured more carefully to distinguish between Pentecostal and Pentecostal.

Second, a host of objections raised against my first effort to elucidate this subject sent me back to re-examine Scripture. They spurred me to engage in further reading of what Pentecostals of various types have published, and to enter into further discussions with them as well. In the outcome I am more confirmed than ever in the basic thesis set forth in the past. I have laboured to state that position more clearly where it had been misunderstood, to add material where others found the argument lacking, and especially to emphasize the essential Biblical points.

Still, I do not imagine that this little work says all that is needed on the subject. It is a popular and limited treatment of Pentecostalism, neither profound in scholarship, nor exhaustive in scope. It is written with a pastor's limited experience, and yet with a pastor's concern that the common man may not be left without plain, practical and sound Biblical guidance on a topic of great importance to him.

I would like to give special thanks to Paul Helm, whose counsel has been of great help to me. Then, thanks to Iain Murray whose patient labours contribute to every work published by the Banner. Finally, thanks to God for a wife who not only patiently bears with the lengthy discourtesy of a husband who is utterly distracted while in the birth pangs of writing, but also encourages him in the work.

May the God who is rich in mercy grant that this labour be not in vain in the Lord. He alone is mighty to the pulling down of strongholds of error.

August 1976   WALTER J. CHANTRY
Grace Baptist Church,
Carlisle,
Pennsylvania.

1: REPORTS OF SIGNS
AND WONDERS

Protestantism is being shaken seriously by the charismatic movement. For centuries there have been small groups claiming to possess the gifts of prophecy and miracle-working but historically Christians have looked upon them as false sects or extremists.[1]

The dawn of the twentieth century served also as the dawn of the Pentecostal Churches. Due to the general apostasy to liberalism early in this century, Pentecostals received a reluctant and cautious acceptance as evangelicals. Their beliefs in a supernatural God and a divinely inspired Word made them helpful allies of fundamentalism.

Since the Second World War the experience of 'miraculous' phenomena has spread beyond the Pentecostal Churches and the movement has gained momentum rapidly. What are frequently known as 'full gospel' practices have now infiltrated most denominations. In recent days 'the charismatic revival', as friends call it, has gained enormous prestige. Indeed, most Christians hesitate to label it unorthodox or unbiblical.

[1] Roman Catholicism has allowed a place for wonder-working by her 'saints'. But Protestantism has stood firmly against admitting that modern miracles of men are from God.

Few religious issues universally interest Americans, but the dramatic 'miracles' of today do. Secular news media have not failed to report the sensational claims to tongues and healing. Pastors frequently are asked their opinions on these phenomena even by those otherwise uninterested in religion. It is one of the first questions met during pastoral visitation. Even sceptics are curious.

In the churches large numbers of laymen have sought and received the 'gifts'. Their search has been encouraged by societies outside of the church. Yet in such groups they have found themselves next to clergymen who are spearheading the movement. Laymen who 'have gotten it' are delivering exciting reports to their Christian friends, encouraging them to share in 'the blessings of Pentecost'.

Those who have been Christians for years are suddenly claiming to have extraordinary gifts and experiences. Few churches have escaped this startling impact. Even the cautious are puzzled by the multiplied reports of supernatural events. What are church members to think of them?

Evangelical societies seem quite vulnerable to this neo-pentecostal thrust. Most have attempted to remain neutral on the issues of tongues and healing. Since societies which do not officially encourage the signs and wonders of this century do not resist them, they most often possess a few officers or leaders who testify to having gifts of miraculous quality, and recently many societies in the United States have moved decidedly towards a pentecostal position.

Student organizations are especially prone to the 'charismatic' spell. Students are often debating the value of such experiences. And even schools are being swept by exciting waves of 'charisma'.

The leading evangelical periodicals either favour the movement or attempt to remain editorially neutral. Virtually every evangelical book store enthusiastically circulates such pentecostal works as *The Cross and the Switchblade* with no embarrassment.[2]

Mission boards are in conflict on the issue. Many boards have personnel who are ardent believers in modern visions, tongues, and healing. A few missions will not send such missionaries to the field; but even these hesitate to condemn neo-pentecostal practices as unbiblical. Their book store ministries circulate pentecostal literature. On the field, pressure for unity among all evangelicals silences any criticism of the movement.

Individual missionaries who have taken a

[2] This same title is on sale in the Roman Catholic Westminster Cathedral, London.

firm stand against modern miracle-workers have found their field churches influenced by zealous apostles of miraculous gifts. Some mission churches are splitting over such practices while others are being completely snatched out of missionary hands by 'full gospel' advocates. At home returning missionaries are confronted with supporting churches increasingly sympathetic to the 'charismatic movement'.

Certainly Protestantism is being challenged to answer serious questions. The Church, the world and perhaps your own conscience are asking, 'What about these things? What does the Bible teach us about tongues and healing?' It will not do to drift along in a vague neutrality. Nor will it do to rest in the seemingly pious but evasive pronouncement, 'I do not wish to oppose a genuine work of God.' The question to be answered is, 'Can this dramatic development of our time be from God?'

The Pentecostals are quite right when they contend that if these are works of the Spirit of God, you dare not shun them. Why not share in these mighty acts? Do you as a Christian not want all of God's blessings? Do you not want your church to be like the New Testament churches?

These are appeals which cannot be ignored. For it is obvious that tongues and miracles were common to churches of Biblical times. They were such ordinary occurrences that members wrote

[4]

about miracles as a matter of course. And certainly supernatural gifts were beneficial to the early church. Why should they not be valuable now?

Again, this twentieth-century movement has adopted a name which demands your attention. It is a challenge. The term 'full gospel' implies that for years the church has been limping along with something like 80 per cent of the gospel. Do you not want *every* benefit Christ has for you and your fellowship of saints? Is not that church most likely to have the presence of God which most resembles the churches of Peter and Paul in experience as well as doctrine?

You dare not ignore the modern claims to miracle working. You may have forced the subject from your mind; but this is not honest. Nor has the issue retreated. Are today's events parallel to those of the Acts? You must review the Scriptures on this pertinent subject to answer these questions.

2: STATING THE
QUESTION PRECISELY

Have you ever attempted to define the word
'miracle'? It is not difficult for the sanctified
mind to see God's power everywhere. Creation
unceasingly provides staggering displays of the
Creator's might. Holy Scripture has taught us
that this world is no independent mechanism.
God's Son is 'upholding all things by the word of
his power' [Hebrews 1:3]. 'By him all things
consist' [Colossians 1:17]. All of the fascinating
majesty of heaven and earth is a mural attesting
his power.

Put a kernel of corn in the ground and it will
multiply 5,000 fold. This is no less wonderful
than five loaves of bread feeding 5,000 men. But
since it is a common occurrence, men take little
notice of it. The birth of a babe is as amazing as
the raising of the dead by Jesus. A non-existent
soul is brought into being by divine power in
conception and birth. It is simply the rarity of
resurrection that makes the rejoining of soul and
body so marvellous to human eyes.

At times Christians use the word 'miracle'
quite loosely as a synonym for 'the supernatural'.
Men speak of 'the miracle of birth' or 'the miracle
of Springtime', because we must stand in awe at
the display of the Creator's power in such events.

Believers also describe the invisible but mighty work of God's grace upon a soul as 'the miracle of the new birth'. This is acceptable as poetic language, for all these things are the direct results of the Almighty's working. Strictly speaking, however, they are not miracles. In a precise definition of the term, we must refer only to works of God which are in the physical realm, uncommon to human experience, and unexplainable in terms of the physical secondary agents.[1] Usual workings of God in this world may be quite as much the effects of God's power as are miracles, but to be accurate we must refer to his normal acts as providence rather than miracle.

Normal events of providence reveal the glory of God, but sin has blinded mortal eyes to it. In wicked rebellion, sinners shut their eyes to this constant revelation of the supernatural. God, then, has done unusual works of power to startle sinners, demand attention and elicit admission of his greatness. The same power veiled in the regular operations of God in providence is unveiled in miracles.

But it is incorrect to say that miracles are violations of natural laws. Though miraculous powers are above or beyond the forces which our Maker employs in our daily experience, they are

[1] For a more exact definition of the word 'miracle' see Richard C. Trench's *Notes on the Miracles of our Lord.*

not in conflict with providential power. A miracle marks an interruption of God's normal pattern of working by his extraordinary act.

It is also wrong to say that a miracle is God's acting without means. Sometimes a miracle is the unveiling of God's power without an intermediate agent – as when he destroyed Sodom. But sometimes it is the unveiling of his might by producing an effect wholly disproportionate to the normal result of a means – as when he opened the Red Sea through Moses' lifting a rod above the water.

Miracles, then, are the extraordinary works of God's power which demand the awed attention of men. And there is no Biblical reason to limit God to performing miracles at certain seasons only. No doubt God is yet executing unusual feats of power. In response to the prayers of his people, God is healing in sovereign power some whom modern medicine has pronounced hopeless. A few theologians prefer to call these events 'acts of extraordinary providence' rather than miracles. But this distinction is likely to escape most minds. Whatever way we choose to describe the fact, it is plain that God's working of wonders cannot be limited to ages past.

'Charismatic' enthusiasts, however, are not merely claiming that *God* is doing miracles in the twentieth century. They are asserting that some twentieth-century *men* have power to perform miracles. No Christian denies that God is doing extraordinary things today, such as marvellously healing the sick. The point of debate is whether the church of the '70's should have *men* able to work miracles.

In other ages God conferred upon certain men the power of performing miracles on his behalf. So enormous was this endowment in the case of Peter that anyone coming under his shadow was likely to be healed of disease. The question of our inquiry is not, 'Should God be working miracles today?' It is rather, 'Should *men* be doing miracles on behalf of God?' It is imperative that this distinction be kept in mind throughout any discussion of the 'full gospel' movement.

3: MIRACLE-WORKERS
SENT FROM GOD

Scripture has a great wealth of information about men endued with power to work wonders. Who were they? And why were they possessed of such amazing gifts? It is the Bible alone that can offer adequate guidelines to our thinking and enable us to evaluate modern claims to tongues and healing.

Old Testament Miracles

Joseph was the first person to receive extraordinary gifts from God, so far as the Biblical record is concerned. This man of God was evidently a prophet. He could give divinely-inspired interpretations of dreams, predicting the future course of history. All of his gifts were directly involved in prophesying, that is, in delivering divinely-revealed truth.

Moses was the first miracle-working *man* of whom we read in the Bible. As a matter of fact, he holds first place throughout the Old Testament in the élite school of those who worked miracles. 'And there arose not a prophet since in Israel like unto Moses ... in all the signs and the wonders, which the Lord sent him to do in the land of Egypt ...' [Deuteronomy 34:10–11].

Why did God send Moses to do wonders? Exodus 4:1–5 gives us an explicit answer to that question. Moses was hesitant to approach the Hebrews in Egypt with the Word of God. After all, he had miserably failed to gain their respect as a leader when he killed an unjust taskmaster. His complaint to God was that they would not believe that he was really a prophet sent from the Almighty. Moses could envisage the scene when he arrived in Egypt and said, 'The God of your fathers hath sent me unto you' [3:13]. 'They won't believe it. They will think I'm an impostor', he thought. 'They will say, The Lord hath not appeared unto thee' [4:1].

It was for just such a contingency that God gave Moses the power to work miracles: 'That they may believe that the Lord God of their fathers ... hath appeared unto thee' [4:5]. Miracle-working powers were credentials to prove that Moses was a prophet sent from God with a divinely-revealed message. The wonders were God's testimonies that Moses indeed spoke the word of truth. This principle universally applies to Old Testament miracles. Only those who were inspired of God to speak his Word were wonder-workers. It was a gift exclusively held by prophets.

This is not to say that attesting to the divine commission of prophets is the only purpose of miracles. God's mighty works also reveal the nature of his saving work. Thus they contain a message in themselves. Yet primarily they were signs and wonders drawing attention to the word of the prophets, without which the marvellous events would puzzle rather than instruct.

Some have thought that judges, as Samson and Shamgar, are exceptions to the rule that only prophets had the power to work miracles. However, such a conclusion is by no means evident. Though sacred history records only the heroic, and at times miraculous, deeds of these men, the history is incomplete. While less fully recorded, we are told that these judges not only delivered the people from oppression, but also governed the people as well. [Judges 2:16–19]. The judges were national leaders [Deut. 17:9] to whom the populace was to resort in difficult matters of jurisprudence. At least in this sense judges like Samson were the heirs to a Mosaic position of national rule. When Joshua occupied such a position he was from time to time an instrument of divine communication, or prophecy, as when the sin of Achan had to be uncovered and when it was time to renew the covenant with Israel near his death. When Samuel, the last and greatest of the judges, appears on the stage of history, he is most notably a prophet. Those who had need of a divine revelation sought him out, as did Saul when he was searching for his father's asses. To say that all judges between Joshua and Samuel spoke prophetically would be to assert more than can be proved from Scripture. But to expect that the Lord had his prophets through this period of dim revelation is not an extravagant dream. That the people of God should have a strictly secular ruler was a shocking concept to Samuel. Was this because all former judges were also prophets, though of lesser stature than he?

When Elijah stood on Mount Carmel to call fire from heaven to consume his sacrifice, he was interested in validating his prophetic ministry. He prayed, 'Lord God of Abraham, Isaac, and of Israel, let it be known this day that thou art God in Israel, *and that I am thy servant, and that I have done all these things at thy word*' [1 Kings 18:36]. He considered the miracle as a confirmation to the people that the man by whom it came was a prophet of God. Elijah was not motivated by personal ambition or desire for acclaim. But the prophet earnestly wanted the multitudes to hearken to the inspired Word which called them to repent.

Psalm 74:9 is an important text on this subject. In the midst of complaints that God's people were desolate, the psalmist said, 'We see not our signs: there is no more any prophet: neither is there among us any that knoweth how long.' Hebrew poetry is known for its parallel phrases which express synonymous ideas in a slightly different way. The poetic verse before us has three parallel phrases, each expressing the same basic idea, but each adding a bit more to the thought. In other words, the absence of signs is equivalent to the absence of a prophet, which in turn is the same as having no authoritative answer to their question, 'How long will God be absent from us?' This is a striking endorsement of the principle that only prophets work miracles. Where miracles are performed we should expect to hear the inspired Word of God spoken. When there is no prophet, there are no signs.

Messianic Miracles

New Testament miracles serve precisely the same end as those of the old covenant. The evidence for this is overwhelming. Jesus performed many miracles to prove that he was the great prophet promised in Deuteronomy 18:15: 'The Lord thy God will raise up unto thee a prophet from the midst of thee, of thy brethren, like unto me; unto him ye shall hearken'. Jesus alone was 'like unto Moses' in wonder-working. Indeed his signs surpassed even those mighty miracles of Moses. Though many mercies were conferred upon men through Christ's miracles, their primary purpose was not to bring compassionate aid to society. They served first and foremost to call attention to the divine authority of his teaching. Though great truths are wrapped up in Jesus' miraculous acts, they could not be understood without his prophetic utterances to which they attested.

John views his Gospel as a catalogue of the signs of Jesus Christ. 'Many other signs truly did Jesus in the presence of his disciples, which are not written in this book: But these are written . . . [John 20:30,31]. Why were his miracles recordded? 'That ye might believe that Jesus is the Christ.' That readers might see that he is the Messiah, the greatest of all prophets, and that they might receive his words as words of life.

In just this way our holy Lord spoke of his own wonders: 'If I do not the works of my Father, believe me not. But if I do, though ye believe not me, believe the works: that ye may know, and believe, that the Father is in me, and I in him' [John 10:37, 38]. Our Lord directed attention to his mighty acts as a validation of his authority as a prophet.

Though many were blind in the face of the mighty signs performed by Jesus, many did conclude from them that he was a prophet. A man named Nicodemus had some theological questions which disturbed him and he decided that Jesus could give him authoritative answers. Thus he approached our Lord saying, 'Rabbi, we know that thou art a teacher come from God' [John 3:2].

How did a scholar of Scripture come to such a conclusion? What led him to place confidence in the words of Jesus? The afore-mentioned text gives us the ground of his conclusion: 'For no man can do these miracles that thou doest, except God be with him'. He was confident that Christ could clear up his questions with authoritative information because he worked miracles.

After Jesus fed 5,000 miraculously, the people who observed the sign concluded correctly, 'This is of a truth that prophet that should come into the world' [John 6:14]. They knew that only prophets performed miracles. A crowd reasoned in precisely the same way in John 7:31: 'Many of the people believed on him, and said, When Christ cometh, will he do more miracles than these which this man hath done?' Having witnessed his mighty works, they were utterly convinced that he must speak the truth and be the Christ. The Christ would do the greatest miracles; for he was expected to speak truth most fully and most plainly. 'When he is come, he will tell us all things' [John 4:25].

That this was the central significance of Jesus' miracles in the minds of his disciples is clear from Peter's sermon on the day of Pentecost. The apostle rebuked the Jews who crucified our Lord for not having believed in him. Their unbelief was inexcusable. 'Jesus of Nazareth, a man

approved of God among you' [Acts 2:22]. How did
the Father testify to them that Christ was a
messenger approved by God? 'By miracles and
wonders and signs, which God did by him in the
midst of you.' Peter was saying to his vast
audience that Jesus' miracles demanded that they
sit at his feet for instruction. But refusing to
acknowledge his evident credentials as a prophet,
they crucified the Lord of Glory.

Apostolic Miracles
New Testament miracles performed by men other
than Jesus also confirmed the authority of prophets
who were spokesmen of God's infallible Word.
In 2 Corinthians 12:12 Paul calls miracles 'signs
of an apostle'. In the context he is giving an
apology for his own apostolic authority. 'Truly the
signs of an apostle were wrought among you in
all patience, in signs, and wonders, and mighty
deeds.' He considered miraculous gifts as God-
given proof of an apostolic ministry. Apostleship
involved being an instrument of divine revelation;
for apostles were authoritative spokesmen for God
and authors of Scripture in the new covenant as
prophets were in the old.

In Galatians 3:5 Paul appealed to his miracle-
working power as evidence that he, rather than
the Judaizers, ought to be believed. He had come
with the gospel working miracles. Those who

sought to force the church back into the old covenant did no wonders. Thus the church was absurd in forsaking Paul for new teachers. Again in Romans 15:18, 19 Paul rehearses God's wonders done through himself as proof of his apostleship.

Hebrews 2:1–4 is vital to an understanding of the Christian doctrine of miracles. In chapter 1 of the epistle it was shown that Jesus is a greater prophet than any other. In the past God had spoken at various times and in diverse ways; but now he has spoken in his own Son – a far superior revelation. Hence chapter 2 begins, 'Therefore we ought to give the more earnest heed to the things which we have heard.' We ought to give careful attention and obedience to the message delivered to us. For if those who heard lesser prophets were judged for ignoring the Old Testament message, how shall we escape condemnation for slighting the words of God's Son?

Then verse 4 brings miracles to our attention. The message to which we must give heed 'began to be spoken by the Lord' himself. However, it was 'confirmed unto us by them that heard him'. First-hand witnesses or apostles who had personally 'companied with us all the time that the Lord Jesus went in and out among us' [Acts 1:21] had a confirming ministry. And Hebrews 2:4 tells us, 'God also (was) bearing them witness, both with signs and wonders, and with divers miracles, and

gifts of the Holy Ghost, according to his own will.'
Again New Testament miracles are viewed in
Scripture itself as God's stamp of approval upon
the message of the apostles, which was an
inspired record of the things they had seen and
heard while with Jesus. Recalling these wonders
should deepen our respect for the authority of
their words and prompt us to give the more
careful heed.

But what of the ordinary Christians by whom
miracles were done in the New Testament
church? Though the apostles were the chief
wonder-workers, many others shared in the gifts
of prophecy, healing, etc. The Book of Acts and
1 Corinthians 12–14 indicate a great range of
extraordinary gifts exercised by many in the
early church.

An incident recorded for us in the Book of Acts
directly links wonders worked by Christians who
were not apostles, with apostolic authority. In
Acts 8:4–13 we find Philip doing miracles and
preaching the gospel in Samaria. Many believed
on Christ and were baptized in consequence of his
ministry. When exciting reports of the conversions were published in Jerusalem, Peter and
John were dispatched to strengthen the work.

After the apostles reached Samaria they prayed
that the converts might receive the Holy Ghost.
Certainly the true converts among them already

had God's Spirit in their hearts, for 'If any man have not the Spirit of Christ, he is none of his' [Romans 8:9]. However, through prayer and the laying on of the apostles' hands, the Spirit came upon the new converts with miraculous gifts. This interpretation may be borne out by the immediate reaction of Simon. He could *see* that they had received the Spirit. He sought to buy apostolic power to transmit the Spirit by the laying on of hands.

We must ask, 'Why could not Philip convey these extraordinary gifts?' He had miracle-working powers himself. But it appears to have been the prerogative of apostles alone to minister these gifts to others. Every recorded instance of men in the church receiving such gifts occurred under the direct ministry of an apostle. Thus even the general exercise of miraculous powers within the church served as a testimony to the prophetic authority of the apostles.

Simon recognized at once that the mighty signs of others attested the unique authority of the apostles, and he sought to buy his way into that élite band. All who did miracles by the power of God did so by the laying on of apostles' hands. Other miracle-workers such as Philip could not transmit the gifts.

Scripture does tell us of miraculous works done by false prophets. But even in Satan's realm, the wonders are intended to secure belief of a message spoken by the worker. That is why they are called 'lying wonders' [2 Thessalonians 2:9]. They deceive men into believing the lies of false teachers. The New Testament indicates that we may expect a continuation of false prophets with their deceitful signs. There shall even be many false christs.

It is an inescapable conclusion of Biblical study that no true servant of Christ will be given power to work miracles unless he is directly associated with prophecy. Whenever we see *men* working miracles by the Spirit of God, we will expect an inspired communication of God's words to attend them. Miracles are God's attestation to the divine mission of those who bring his fresh revelations to us. We are compelled to look upon the men who work wonders and transmit the ability to others not merely as preachers, but as the very prophets of God.

The Biblical evidence requires us to amend our questions. We may *not* merely ask, 'Should men be doing miracles in the church today?' To ask that question is in reality to ask, 'Should there be prophets in the church today? Should men be directly delivering the revealed truth of God to us?' Certainly we expect men to preach the Word revealed by the apostles and prophets. But are we to look for further revelation in our day?

4: IS SCRIPTURE
COMPLETE?

A Pertinent Question

Let there be no mistaking the central thrust of
the 'charismatic revival', it is offering the Church
a new approach to authority and absolute truth.
Most prominent among the wonders of the
modern pentecostal movement are 'speaking in
tongues', 'prophecy', 'dreams', and 'visions'.
None of these gifts may be conceived of apart
from the concept of an infallible revelation from
God delivered to us through those who are
experiencing the gifts.

'Speaking in tongues' is nothing less than to
have one's speech faculties so completely control-
led by the Holy Ghost that a man utters a language unknown to himself. The words are not
consciously chosen by the speaker, rather he
speaks the very words of God. Regardless of the
language used, speaking in tongues *is* a form of
prophecy.[1] Because King Saul once uttered
ecstatic speech, it became a proverb in Israel, 'Is

[1] The word 'prophecy' is most often used in Scripture for any
spoken word from God. Occasionally, as in 1 Cor. 14, it is
used in a more technical sense. There it refers to delivery of
a divine revelation in a language commonly understood by
its hearers. And there it is distinguished from speaking in
tongues. But both are forms of divine communication to
man.

Saul also among the prophets?' [1 Samuel 10:12].
Anyone who speaks in this manner must be
identified as an agent of divine revelation.
Certainly visions and dreams from God are claims
to receiving inspired communications of God's
truth.

In contemporary Pentecostalism even the gift
of healing serves to enhance the authority of the
one who has the gift. Great numbers believe the
opinions of those who perform wonders because
their 'gifts' indicate that 'they are filled with the
Spirit'. The implication of such logic is clear. How
can anyone question the doctrines of miracle-
workers? Even if one were to reason from the
Scriptures, he would have no miracles to support
his position. Many prefer to trust the teachings of
men because of their 'gifts'. 'Can a man be teaching false doctrine when he does such mighty
things?, ask the captivated.

A survey of 'charismatic' meetings reveals a
very low esteem for God's Word. Those who
attend are more elated over the words of the
twentieth-century prophets than over the inscripturated words of Christ and his apostles. It is the
message in tongues or of prophecy that thrills
participants with the conviction that God has
spoken to them in their meetings.

As the 'gifts' increase, exposition of God's
Word decreases. Meetings are filled with 'sharing

experiences' but with only an occasional reference to the holy Word of God. Many who have been drawn after this movement are woefully untaught in the first things of the faith through a neglect of the Word. They live on visible, emotional experiences and not upon truth. Even some who spend hours perusing the Bible do so not for the purpose of grasping truth but in the hope of inducing a new thrill in their truth-parched souls.

There is no question but that the 'charismatic' groups have added their new revelations to the Bible as infallible truth revealed from God, as is seen in the testimony of David J. du Plessis, who for years was secretary of the World Conference of Pentecostal Churches, which gathers representatives of the vast majority of Pentecostals throughout the world. Probably there is no one more directly responsible for the proliferation of charismatic influence in denominational circles. He begins his book *The Spirit Bade Me Go*[2] with the explanation that his book is basically tape-recorded messages which he later edited. His attitude towards his own book is revealed in such statements as these: 'It was my privilege to edit and prepare for publication in this form those revelations that I received from Him while ministering in conferences . . .' 'Friends have pleaded with

[2] Logos International Foundation Trust, London, 1970.

me to put into print the things I have said, or rather those things that the Holy Ghost has said through me. To attempt to write about these things would not be quite the same as quoting more directly the utterances made under the unction of the Spirit.' Although he notes that the Lord intended his messages for specific conferences, and thus I suppose he would deny that they are to be canonized, he remarks: 'I am sure we can all learn from what the Spirit has had to say to others.' Where the leaders so forthrightly claim to speak a 'Thus saith the Lord', it is not surprising that their young followers do not hesitate to impose their sayings upon brethren with insistence that their discernment, knowledge, guidance, judgment, or exhortation come directly from the Spirit with all the authority and incontrovertible force of heaven. Furthermore, without such claims, there can be no pretending to possess many of the gifts listed in 1 Cor. 12.

I know that some pentecostal leaders would heartily deny that contemporary revelations are infallible truth to be equated with Scripture in their authority, but it is the essential impression necessarily conveyed by any claim to the 'gifts'.

Historically Christians have believed that the Bible is the *only* standard of faith and practice. Opposition to miracle-working, tongues-speaking cults has been based upon this high regard for

Scripture. Our doctrine of Scripture gives us confidence in the *unique authority* and *absolute sufficiency* of Scripture whereby the Holy Spirit guides our minds into truth, directs our lives in this world, and brings us to satisfying heart-communion with God. This conviction necessarily implies that God is not giving further revelation through prophets today.

As the Westminster Confession of Faith so accurately states the view of most Protestants through the centuries – 'The whole counsel of God, concerning all things necessary for his own glory, man's salvation, faith, and life, is either expressly set down in Scripture, or by good and necessary consequence may be deduced from Scripture: *unto which nothing at any time is to be added, whether by new revelations of the Spirit, or traditions of men.*' [Chapter 1, Article VI] – we believe that no further revelation from God is to be expected. The Old and New Testaments are complete and sufficient for all our needs. The Bible *alone* is our authority!

'Charismatic' enthusiasts are undermining confidence in the sufficiency of Scripture. Direct revelation in prophecy and tongues is sought for edification. Some would deny that their new messages add anything to the existing canon of Scripture. They only receive direction as to what portion of God's Word should be called to the attention of the church at the moment. Or they only receive warnings of providential calamity. Or they only receive specific guidance in personal or church affairs. Nevertheless it is a fresh message from heaven which provides the desired guidance, not the Scriptures.

Pentecostal practice is a *de facto* denial of the sufficiency of Scripture. Neo-pentecostal enthusiasts are implying that the Bible is not able to make a man 'thoroughly furnished unto all good works' [2 Timothy 3:17]. They are not simply seeking the Spirit's enlightenment in the study of God's Word. They are seeking an additional word from God, a further source of truth. For them the Bible is not enough. Expecting a new message from heaven, Pentecostals believe that new prophets are abroad in the land today.

Even amongst those who have not reached that conclusion there is sometimes to be found an attitude towards miracles which amounts to a lack of confidence in God's Word. This may be seen, for instance, in Henry W. Frost's book *Miraculous Healing*. Discussing his expectation that miracles will increase, Frost remarks: 'It may confidently be anticipated, as the present apostasy increases, that Christ will manifest his deity and lordship in increasing measure through miracle-signs, including healings. *We are not to say, therefore, that the Word is sufficient*. It is so to those who know and believe it; but it is not so to those who have never heard of it, or who, having heard, have disbelieved it. To these persons, a dramatic appeal may have to be made, and on the plane where such will most easily be understood, namely, the physical. The missionary abroad, therefore, may have it in mind, in a case of the sickness of others, that God may choose to make him a miracle-worker'.[3]

Few adherents to modern miracle-working by men have been so mild in their views as Dr. Frost. Yet here is an explicit denial of the sufficiency of Scripture for evangelism. It is to be feared that such attitudes run very deep within the 'charismatic revival.' Men have forgotten that it was our Lord who said, 'If they hear not Moses and the prophets, neither will they be persuaded, though one rose from the dead' [Luke 16:31]. Many today go beyond Dr. Frost in seeking an additional word, not merely a fresh sign to make the Bible believable. But in either case there is a definite lack of confidence in God's holy Word.

But where did our spiritual forefathers find their dogma that we are not to expect new revelations from the Spirit in our age? Whence comes the opinion that the Scriptures are utterly sufficient as a standard of truth and as a source to guide us in *all* practical matters? In hearing the

[3] pp. 109, 110 (italics mine).

Pentecostals speak upon this subject, one receives the impression that this old Protestant doctrine is a relic of the Roman Catholic system. The Reformers did not go far enough in extracting the church from the Stygian darkness of medieval theology. Now the new forces have arisen to complete the Reformation, to give the church the 'full gospel'.

Quite to the contrary, Roman Catholic corruptions arose from the proliferation of authorities additional to Scripture. The Roman Church lifted to the plane of Scripture the visions of her members and the decrees of her popes. It is this departure from adherence to the Scripture alone which has led to every evil of the Roman Church. On the other hand the most fundamental element of the Reformation was the cry of 'Sola Scriptura' from students of the Bible. The 'charismatic movement' does not carry on the Reformation, but rather strikes a damaging blow to its very roots. They would destroy the Protestant foundation of confiding in Scripture alone.

An Evident Answer

As is clearly evident, our Protestant forefathers drew their dogma directly from the New Testament. Hebrews 1:1-3 contrasts Old Testament prophecy with New Testament revelation. The comparison is intended to display the superiority of New Testament disclosures of truth. Old Testament truth was written at various times during a lengthy era of human history. There was a progressive unfolding of truth through many messengers who lived in widely distant centuries. Again, the Old Testament is marked by differing methods of communicating God's message to man. There were dreams, voices from heaven, angels speaking, etc.

All of this is in marked contrast with the new era of revelation into which we have entered. We have come to 'these last days'. In the first century A.D., when the Epistle to the Hebrews was written, the 'last days' had arrived. The contrast drawn between how the revelation came to 'the fathers' and how it was now finally given, necessarily implies that revelation will no more come gradually through centuries of unfolding, nor through a great host of messengers. As we shall see as we proceed, the revelation of these last days came in one generation; indeed it all came by one Person.

God's revelation of truth reached a glorious climax when Christ was on earth. 'God hath spoken unto us by his Son.' In the person of Jesus Christ revelation had been brought to completion with a dramatic suddenness. God's Son embodies all that the Father has to say to men. Nothing needful was held back for a later time. No greater revelation can be imagined. Christ is the ultimate truth and reveals it fully. He is the brightness of the Father's glory personified. All coverings are removed. He is the express image of the Father's Person – fully and perfectly revealed. He is the grand period or full-stop at the conclusion of God's report to men. The passage breathes unreserved finality. Christ, the Son of God, is the grand finale of revelation.

So complete is he as God's revelation, and so sufficient was his work as a prophet that the apostles and their New Testament books are viewed in Hebrews 2:1–4 as merely confirming what the Great Prophet had already said. Apostolic writings are echoes of what was heard from the lips of our holy Lord. When the Holy Spirit of inspiration came upon them, it was to bring back to their memories what Jesus had taught beforehand and to illumine them concerning the significance of his sayings [John 14:26]. The sun of revelation shone in Jesus Christ. The apostles' writings were not new beams of light, but reflections of the glory that shone in the Son of God.

This view of revelation coming to an end in Jesus Christ pervades other passages in the New Testament. John's Gospel is especially replete with this theme. John 1:1 identifies Jesus as 'The Word' of God. He is God. He is the fullest and most exhaustive expression of God. He is the complete truth of God. Thus he could say in John 14:6 'I am the truth'. He is the whole truth, the last word. John 1:14 indicates that when this Word was made flesh, the apostles saw his glory, 'full of truth'. Other prophets had given us particles of truth. He was *full* of truth. No man has seen God at any time, but the only begotten Son who eternally dwells in the bosom of the Father, he has fully declared the Father [John 1:18]. Anything after the words of Jesus Christ would be anticlimactical. He was the only one qualified to tell men all the truth they can receive about the Father. And he perfectly fulfilled that mission.

John 14:7–10 has a very instructive incident from the life of our Master. Jesus was breaking the news to his disciples that he was going away. To console his devoted friends who had sacrificed everything for the privilege of being with him, our Lord noted that they knew the Father and had seen him. But Philip was not satisfied. In verse 8 he begged for one glorious glimpse of the Father and that would suffice. Perhaps he felt that they had not yet reached the heights of former saints like Moses who gazed on the back parts of the Almighty. If only they could have some such ecstatic experience!

Jesus was most disturbed with Philip's request. 'Have I been so long time with you, and yet hast thou not known me, Philip? he that hath seen me hath seen the Father.' What a withering rebuke! Ought not Philip to have seen all that was to be seen of God's glory? How eagerly Moses would have exchanged his vision to listen to the words of the Son of God! Jesus is the living glory of God, the walking embodiment of his person. Philip's search for something more was an insult to the Son of God.

A similar insult is given by the modern desire for further revelations. It is an indication that seekers of 'charisma' are failing to see the glory of God in the face of Jesus Christ. Though the infallible words of Jesus Christ have been so long time with them, they look for something more in order to know the living God. They are missing the wonder of the truth that the Scripture is the all-sufficient revelation given by the Spirit of God. Some blinded eyes read the very sayings of the Son of God and look away to more exciting prospects.

Would not a vision be more thrilling to Philip than merely talking to God's Son? Would not tongues and dreams be more satisfying today than merely to give attention to the words of the Saviour? We must be as distressed as our Lord. Pentecostals are unconsciously despising the revelation of God in Christ as insufficient. Too often their real lift comes apart from his Word. Their practices cry out, 'There must be something more', or they would give the Word of Christ their devoted attention in their meetings and pray for the Spirit's aid to comprehend it.

When Jesus was about to leave this earth, he prayed to the Father, 'I have finished the work which thou gavest me to do' [John 17:4]. What was the task he had perfectly accomplished? Verse 8 tells us in part, 'I have given unto them the words which thou gavest me.' The indication is that there are no more unspoken words held in reserve for another era. John 15:15 says it more explicitly, '*All* things that I have heard of my Father I have made known unto you.' Just as his cry from the cross, 'It is finished', signified that nothing more needed to be done as priest to secure redemption for his flock, so these comments herald the conclusion of his perfect prophetic ministry.

Before Pentecost the apostles had a deficiency which kept them from the truth. The brightness of the Father's glory shone before them, but they were unprepared to grasp such fulness and finality of truth. They could not comprehend the ultimate in revelation though it was before their very eyes. There was no lack in the transmission of truth. The difficulty was in their personal ability to receive the truth. But the Holy Ghost would come to teach them the things which they had learned from Christ and enable them infallibly to record the same in Scripture. As Jesus promised, 'When he, the Spirit of truth, is come, he will guide you into all truth' [John 16:13]. The Lord kept his promise by giving all revelation to his apostles. Today the church does need a greater measure of the Spirit to understand the words of Christ. For this we must all pray. But she does *not* have need of new messages from heaven.

As our hymn so fittingly remarks:

How firm a foundation, ye saints of the Lord,
Is laid for your faith in his excellent Word!
What more can he say than to you he hath said,
You who unto Jesus for refuge have fled?

What indeed is to be added to Christ, the embodiment of all truth? The church is built upon the sure foundation of the apostles and prophets [Ephesians 2:20]. But the modern 'charismatic' people seem to believe that much was left unsaid by the apostles. 'The foundation of truth must be expanded if the church is to flourish', they tell us.

Absence of a singular esteem for the Scriptures is no slight matter. The lack of complete confidence in the Bible on the part of neo-pentecostals is to be greatly deplored. Failure to see Jesus Christ as the final revelation of truth is a major

[35]

error that will open the door of the church to a multitude of heresies, taught in the name of truth. Every true movement initiated by the Spirit of God leads men back to the words of Christ which were inscripturated by his own inspiration.

Some men have ridiculed an appeal to Revelation 22:18, 19 when discussing the close of the canon (the end to divine messages from the Lord). However, in the context of all that the Bible says about Jesus being the final prophet, the climax of revelation, the words are most significant. It is this same Jesus Christ who speaks in the last chapter of the Bible, 'If any man shall add unto these things, God shall add unto him the plagues that are written in this book.' Our Lord makes this comment in the closing verses of the last confirming witness to his revelation. The Saviour gave his warning through the last living apostle at the conclusion of his ministry.

Some would prefer to weaken our Lord's warning signal by saying that it only applies to the Book of Revelation. But such strong and unusual language must be more than a prohibition to tamper with that one writing. We must see it as did Matthew Henry. He wrote, 'This sanction is like a flaming sword to guard the canon of the Scripture from profane hands.'

Revelation is no usual book. It is a sweeping

analysis of history from the first advent of Christ to the second. Jesus had promised that the Spirit would teach his apostles 'all things' [John 14:26]. The Spirit had come and fulfilled the promise. Apostles had communicated the authoritative word. The task of revelation was finished. The Book of Revelation is the last apostolic word to the church. The Almighty Saviour, seated at God's right hand, opens his sovereign lips personally to declare that nothing is to be added to what has been recorded. Beware of meddling with Christ's revelation! All modern prophecy is spurious! God's truth has come to us in a fixed and finished objective revelation. We must not accept the new 'revelations' of neo-pentecostalism.

5: GIFTS IN THE EARLY CHURCH

Participation in the 'charismatic' trend involves denying the vital doctrine of the unique authority and sufficiency of Scripture. But this conclusion may prompt definite questions in your mind. Why then were charismatic practices in evidence in New Testament churches? Was the early church despising the revelation received from Christ when it practised prophesying and tongues-speaking? Was it denying the unique authority and sufficiency of Scripture? If so, why is it so vital now? And does not an important passage in the Bible, namely 1 Cor. 12–14, indicate that such practices are normal for a true church?

Answers to some of these questions have been implied in former chapters, and they will become more plain by a survey of the Corinthian passage. It is agreed that in the church at Corinth many supernatural or miraculous gifts were exercised. There was 'the word of wisdom', 'the word of knowledge', 'faith', 'healing', 'working of miracles', 'prophecy', 'discerning of spirits', 'divers kinds of tongues', 'interpretation of tongues' (1 Cor. 12:8–10) most of which involved divine revelation. They were manifestations of the Spirit. Indeed this did deny the *unique* authority of Scripture. The Bible was not the *only* verbally inspired word to that church, which also received

God's truth through these gifts.

Furthermore such a method of edifying the saints at Corinth denied the sufficiency of Scripture as it then existed, and for good reason. The Saviour had come. The New Testament Church had been formed. The children of God were no longer living under the Old Covenant. Yet the New Testament had not been written. The full revelation of truth in Jesus Christ had not yet been given to the church in writing by 'them that heard him'. [Hebrews 2:3]. It was not good for an entire generation of the servants of God to live isolated from the magnificent grace and truth which come by Jesus Christ, while the various books of the New Testament were being written and collected. Hence stop-gap revelations were given to edify the church while the Holy Ghost brought all things of Christ to the remembrance of the Apostles [John 14:26]. Believers must live on Christ before the apostles could make him fully known.

During the period when the New Testament was being written, the above-mentioned gifts exercised in the apostolic churches would serve as signs by which God bore witness to the divine authority of the apostles. It was they who brought extraordinary spiritual gifts to the churches through the laying on of hands, and as exercised in the churches the gifts in turn witnessed to the authority of those who wrote the New Testament.

The gifts of prophecy and tongues in apostolic time had an opposite effect from their modern counterparts. The existence of miraculous gifts in the early church pays honour to the completed Scriptures. The apostolic message inscripturated in the New Testament is so vital that the church cannot live without it. While it was being written, the same truths must more or less be given in another fashion to edify the church. And the miraculous exercise of gifts bears witness to the profound importance of the apostolic mission in confirming what Jesus began to speak. [Heb. 2:3]. Hence those miracles witnessed to the unique authority and sufficiency of the Scripture when complete.

However, since the completion of the New Testament and the death of the apostles, miracles and revelations have another implication altogether. They now suggest that even the *apostolic* word is insufficient, as tongues and prophecy in the early church did imply that the Old Testament scriptures were insufficient. Since the apostles themselves tell us that they fully revealed Christ, desire for revelation beyond Scripture is a desire to go beyond Christ; it is a declaration that the apostles failed in their mission and that the Holy Spirit by tongues and prophecy must compensate for the deficiencies of

the *apostolic* word. The clear implication is that
the church must be founded upon apostles and
prophets and modern messages as well. If additional revelation is unnecessary, why should the
Spirit give revelatory gifts? Since the Scripture
was completed, its authority is *unique* and its
message *sufficient*. And the Epistle to the Corinthians bears this out.

A Warning

'Now concerning spiritual gifts, brethren, I
would not have you ignorant. Ye know that ye
were Gentiles, carried away unto these dumb
idols, even as ye were led. Wherefore I give you
to understand, that no man speaking by the
Spirit of God calleth Jesus accursed: and that no
man can say that Jesus is the Lord, but by the
Holy Ghost.' (1 Cor. 12:1–3].

Paul began his lesson on gifts to the Corinthian
church with an interesting warning. 'I would not
have you ignorant'. This is a very simple and
basic matter. It is the foundation stone upon
which much will be built. No one will deny that
it is possible to approach the subject of miracles
and extraordinary gifts in a thoughtless manner.
The wiser among Pentecostals themselves recognize that many are swept away with mindless
emotion in so-called 'charismatic' meetings. But
the Christian must be a thinking man. God's

Spirit does not dull the intellect. He quickens the mind. Believers must not be ignorant on the subject of spiritual manifestations.

Support for this warning comes by way of contrast. Paul reminds the Corinthians of their past experience in occult heathenism. They worshipped idols, lifeless stocks. But Satanic powers were present with a controlling influence over men. Many were compelled to yield. It was an irrational force. That is the significance of the terms 'carried away' and 'led'[1] in the light of the contrast. Meetings swayed by senseless emotion are not of God. It is the way of devils to give men unintelligent feelings and to carry them along in extraordinary activity which the mind cannot comprehend. Here is a solemn warning to any Christian in a confused generation. At all meetings keep an intelligent, discerning mind about you. Some will suggest that logic is cold. But the senseless is Satanic.

A scale is given us in verse 3 by which to evaluate various spirits. Note that it is a doctrinal yardstick. Particularly ask what a spirit says concerning Jesus Christ. Immediately 1 John 4:1 & 2 will come to mind: 'Beloved, believe not every spirit, but try the spirits whether they are of God . . .' Much more will be said on this matter in

[1] See Charles Hodge for comparison of this word with 'led by the Spirit of God'. (Exposition of First Ep. to Corinthians p. 240).

chapter 8. The test is not feelings but scrutiny by truth. David J. du Plessis forgot this. In *The Spirit Bade Me Go*, Logos, 1970, he testified: 'Twenty-four ecumenical leaders were comfortably seated around me . . . I could remember days when I had wished I could have set my eyes upon such men to denounce their theology and pray the judgment of God upon them for what I considered their heresies and false doctrines. Here was such an opportunity and they said, "Be devastatingly frank." I prayed, "Lord, what would you have me to do?"

'That morning something happened to me. After a few introductory words I suddenly felt a warm glow come over me. I knew this was the Holy Spirit taking over, but what was He doing to me? Instead of the old harsh spirit of criticism and condemnation in my heart, I now felt such love and compassion for these ecclesiastical leaders that I would rather have died for them than pass sentence upon them. All at once I knew that the Holy Spirit was in control and I was beside myself and yet sober as a judge. [2 Cor. 5:13]. Thank God, from that day on I knew what it meant to minister along the "more excellent way" [1 Cor. 12:31]. This indeed is the technique of the Holy Spirit.' (p. 16). From that day du Plessis never appeared to rebuke liberals for departures from the truth. He became their friend and told them, 'the church does not need better theologians but rather men full of faith and of the Holy Ghost.' (p. 18). This calls to mind the sad word of Psalm 78:9: 'The children of Ephraim, being armed, and carrying bows, turned back in the day of battle.'

With doctrinal alertness, most charismatic meetings would be quickly shunned. It is through ignorance that this tide gains momentum. May it echo in believers' ears, 'I would not have you ignorant'!

General Principles About Gifts

'Are all apostles? Are all prophets? Are all teachers? Are all workers of miracles? Have all the gifts of healing? Do all speak with tongues? Do all interpret?' [1 Cor. 12:29, 30].

Through the rest of chapter 12 the church is likened to one body, with Jesus Christ the common Head, the Holy Spirit enlivening each member. All manifestations of the Spirit and all ministries are for the common good [v. 7]. Next Paul stresses the diversity of members, that is, diversity in their gifts and ministry, a teaching that effectively undermines a major premise of Pentecostals.

Many neo-pentecostals believe it is possible for a person to be baptized in the Spirit without speaking in tongues. Any of the gifts listed in the chapter may signify the baptism. Pentecostals insist that tongues is *the* proof of having received this experience. At least on this point neo-pentecostals are nearer to the Biblical position. In verse 30 Paul asks, 'Do all speak with tongues?' The obvious answer is 'No, all do not speak with tongues'. The 'all' in view are all the members of the Spirit-baptized body [verse 13]. Pentecostals attempt to skirt this clear declaration of Paul by saying that the question is really, 'Do all speak with tongues in church gatherings?' But that is not the question. Paul does not even address himself to public services until chapter 14. The 'all' of verse 30 signifies the members of the body, which Christians continue to be whether gathered for public worship or not. This text alone makes unbiblical the doctrine of Pentecostals that all Spirit-baptized believers manifest their baptism by speaking in tongues. Pentecostals are in direct conflict with Paul's point that the manifestations of the Spirit in the body are quite varied. All do not speak with tongues any more than all exercise the office of apostle [verse 29].

Gifts No Sign of Grace

'Though I speak with the tongues of men and of angels, and have not charity, I am become as sounding brass, or a tinkling cymbal. And though I have the gift of prophecy, and understand all mysteries, and all knowledge; and though I have all faith, so that I could remove mountains, and have not charity, I am nothing. And though I bestow all my goods to feed the poor, and though I give my body to be burned, and have not charity, it profiteth me nothing' [1 Cor. 13:1–3].

Upon reaching 1 Cor. 13, Paul sets forth a truth which strikes at the root of all branches of modern charismatic teaching. Here the father of the Corinthian Church teaches that miraculous gifts are no sign whatsoever of spiritual health in the one who possesses them. It is possible to speak with tongues, prophesy, exercise faith (the gift), sacrificially give and suffer, and yet be nothing. There are examples in Scripture of men who had extraordinary gifts but who were utterly void of God's grace. Judas is a prime example. Our Lord emphasized the sad delusion which arises from imagining that spiritual gifts evidence spiritual well-being in a man's soul. This he did in Matthew 7:22 & 23: 'Many will say to me in that day, Lord, Lord, have we not prophesied in thy name? and in thy name have cast out devils? and in thy name done many wonderful works? And then will I profess unto them, I never knew you: depart from me, ye that work iniquity'. Many perform miracles in this world only to perish in the next.

Paul alluded to this possibility in 12:2 by

reminding the Corinthians that even pagans have amazing manifestations of power. Now in 13:1–3 he nails down the point that outward spiritual gifts furnish no index whatsoever to the spiritual state of a man. Rather, inward spiritual graces, carved upon the soul, are the signs of spiritual greatness. Not the Spirit's gifts but the Spirit's fruits are the gauge of holiness, of usefulness to the Lord, and of spiritual prosperity in the soul. Pre-eminently love is the test. Gifts at Corinth were not given as signs to assure the church of its health and vigour. They were given, as Paul said in chapter 12, to edify the whole body.

What would happen to the charismatic trend if it no longer taught and suggested that miraculous gifts were a sign of spiritual well-being? This is the key to the whole outlook of the movement. David du Plessis himself admits that Pentecostals lose their effectiveness when they stop insisting that tongues are a sign of spiritual blessedness, a sign of the baptism in the Spirit. All charismatics, including the most mild, look upon various acts of power and public gifts as a sign of a special presence of the Spirit. God's Word tells us it is possible to produce all the gifts without love. It is possible to have gifts and be nothing. Graces, not gifts, are signs of spiritual vitality. They are found within, not in any outward demonstrations of charismata.

Love in Exercising Gifts

'Charity suffereth long, and is kind; charity envieth not; charity vaunteth not itself, is not puffed up, doth not behave itself unseemly, seeketh not her own, is not easily provoked, thinketh no evil: rejoiceth not in iniquity, but rejoiceth in the truth: beareth all things, believeth all things, hopeth all things, endureth all things' [1 Cor. 13:4–7].

As Paul describes love in verses 4–7, he is not speaking in the context of marital love. He has no general reference. His specific application is to a confused church exercising many spiritual gifts, but more in need of spiritual grace. You can find love by watching for patience and meekness [verse 4]. Love will never act in a fanatical manner (the meaning of 'behave itself unseemly') nor seek merely personal ends [v. 5]. Love hates sin and rejoices in the truth [v. 6]. It is interested in holiness and doctrine (remember 12:3). Again we have profound tests for all charismatic meetings, or Reformed meetings for that matter. Is there shameful behaviour, the promoting of men, the presence of sin, the absence of truth? If so, these meetings are lacking in love. Whatever the gifts, the essence is missing. However spectacular the powers displayed, the loveless gathering or the loveless person is marked by failure.

Gifts Must Depart From The Church

'Charity never faileth: but whether there be prophecies, they shall fail; whether there be tongues, they shall cease; whether there be knowledge, it shall vanish away. For we know in part, and we prophesy in part. But when that which is perfect is come, then that which is in part shall be done away. When I was a child, I spake as a child, I understood as a child, I thought as a child; but when I became a man, I put away childish things. For now we see through a glass darkly; but then face to face; now I know in part: but then shall I know even as also I am known' [1 Cor. 13:8–12].

Verses 8–12 directly address themselves to the impermanence of miraculous gifts in the Church. What we have seen in the rest of Scripture leads us to expect this. But here it is simply and firmly stated. Love is enduring; it will not cease. Never will love depart from the church. But 'prophecies', 'tongues' and 'knowledge' will certainly depart. These are the gifts mentioned in 12:8–10 as 'prophecy', 'the word of knowledge', and 'divers kinds of tongues'. That is what the apostle has in mind. He is comparing miraculous gifts with inward graces. It would be foolish to think that knowledge, language, and truth would ever disappear in the absolute sense of the word. Rather

Paul states that the gifts will vanish from the church.

When and why they must disappear from the church is clearly stated in verses 9–12. Knowledge and prophecy were only partial and imperfect forms of revelation. But there is something 'perfect' coming. At once our minds think of heaven. That is the perfect state. But the word translated 'perfect', in its New Testament usage, does not always mean ideally perfect. The very same word is used again in 1 Corinthians 14:20, where it is translated 'men'. The idea is 'mature' in contrast with 'childish'. That this meaning of the word is intended in 13:10 is quite clear from the continuation of the contrast with 'childish' in verse 11. When fully-matured or adult revelation comes, then the partial revelations of a childish state will be put away.

Certainly the thought of this text must be seen in the light of 2 Timothy 3:16 & 17. 'All scripture is given by inspiration of God . . . that the man of God may be perfect, thoroughly furnished unto all good works.' In neither passage does 'perfect' have in view the glorified man in heaven. It refers to the man completely equipped for life in this world, the man come to full maturity. When Scripture is completed, then the church will have revelation thoroughly suited to her condition on earth. Our completed Bible is perfect in the sense that it is utterly sufficient revelation for all our needs. Paul is saying, 'When the sufficient comes, the inadequate and partial will be done away. Tongues will vanish away, knowledge will cease at the time that the New Testament is finished.'

The amazing gifts catalogued in chapter 12 would only serve for an inferior situation. Their partial usefulness consigned them to a temporary state. But there is no need to cling to these gifts. Does a full-grown man cling to childish speech, understanding and thought [v. 11]? When the man is mature he puts away childish things. Similarly the manly words, thoughts, and satisfying insights of a completed Scripture will cause the church to outgrow the childhood of charismatic revelations.

Furthermore, many have been led astray in commenting on v. 12. Because the contrast appears so stark, they have thought that the reference is to heaven once more. Many commentators have said that Paul is contrasting present knowledge with heavenly understanding. But it is not his concern here to speak of glory. There is no indication that he is talking of heaven. No, the subject is the time and reason for miraculous gifts to cease; 'now' and 'then' have this continual frame of reference.

The fact is that the contrasts of verse 12 are not so absolute as is often supposed. Bible margins have recognized a dependence here on Numbers 12:6–8. Language is quite similar in both passages. The occasion is Jehovah rebuking Miriam and Aaron for speaking against his servant Moses. 'And he said, Hear now my words: If there be a prophet among you, I the Lord will make myself known unto him in a vision, and will speak unto him in a dream. My servant Moses is not so, who is faithful in all mine house. With him will I speak mouth to mouth, even apparently, and not in dark speeches; and the similitude of the Lord shall he behold.' At once we recognize the figures used in 1 Cor. 13:12, a contrast between dim, partial revelation and open, full-faced display of the Lord. Not a contrast between prophet and heaven is before us, but a contrast between lesser and greater prophet.

In the Old Testament, Moses stood as the great prophet who spoke to God 'mouth to mouth, even apparently'. Other prophets received 'dark speeches' and 'similitudes' by the obscure means of 'visions' and 'dreams'. In the New Testament Jesus Christ stands as the great prophet who dwelt in the bosom of the Father and has declared him. His full and complete revelation of the Father was inscripturated by the apostles. Other 'charismatic' revelations were the equivalent of seeing through a glass imperfectly transparent (like Old Testament dreams and visions). They gave only partial disclosure, 'darkly' (that is, 'in a riddle'). By comparison, receiving Scripture was coming 'face to face' with God. It is the 'familiar' approach to God by his Son, Jesus Christ. Verse 12 summarizes the necessity for miraculous gifts to cease! Though cessation was still future when Paul wrote this epistle, it became a thing of the past after John wrote the Book of Revelation. Then the gifts of Chapter 12 were done away!

Chapter 13 concludes with a comment which further shows that verses 8–13 are not contrasting earthly knowledge with heavenly. For even after prophecy and tongues cease, faith and hope will abide. There will be no hope in heaven. 'Hope that is seen is not hope: for what a man seeth, why doth he yet hope for?' (Romans 8:24). But after Scripture is completed, hope will continue in the church until the day of Jesus Christ.

Upon examining the present-day church, one is often distressed with its weakness and 'failure', its sin and coldness. There is no lack of voices saying, 'What we need is to return to the state of the church in apostolic times.' just such reasoning has led to a longing for miraculous gifts. They existed in the infant church. If only we had them now! 'Quite the contrary!', says the apostle. 'You must not desire to return to the childish'. Until Scripture was written, the church was in an inferior position regarding truth. Believers must not seek to go back beyond 100 A.D. and the completed Bible. They must not desire the dark utterances when they have face-to-face truth in Scripture!

1 Cor. 12–14 is not a passage asserting miraculous gifts as a norm for the church of all ages. It prepares the church for these manifestations of the Spirit to cease with the completion of Scripture. What man would revert to a child's apprehension of truth, after tasting the mature and gracious revelation of truth in Scripture? Yet that is what the charismatics ask us to do. They invite us to child's talk and dark riddles after our Lord by his apostles has given us 'face to face' revelation of the Father. Tongues, prophecies, the word of wisdom, and faith were useful enough for the childhood days. But the perfectly suited has come; the manly is here. The temporary gifts have ceased.

Supervision of Temporary Gifts

'For if the trumpet give an uncertain sound, who shall prepare himself to the battle? So likewise ye, except ye utter by the tongue words easy to be understood, how shall it be known what is spoken? for ye shall speak into the air' [1 Cor. 14:8, 9].

Meanwhile the generation in which the Corinthians lived required guidance for the use and exercise of their temporary gifts; so Chapter

14. After the instruction of Chapter 13, it seems rather anti-climactic to study this chapter for our present purposes. Yet some truths bear repetition.

Some Pentecostals have taught that speaking in tongues, whether private or public, is always an act of prayer, usually of praise to God. Whether this is true or not, verses 5, 27 and 28 indicate definitely that tongues must not be used in a public gathering without an interpreter. The great reason for this is the absolute necessity of common edification in worship [vv. 2–19]. And for edification there *must* be understanding. Paul has uncovered again the foundation stone of 12:1–3. No work of the Spirit in edifying is senseless or mindless. That is the devil's way to carry men along. To be built up there must be understanding, however darkly and through glass.

We are never led to expect the Spirit of God graciously to perform his offices in a soul, except in close conjunction with truth. The sovereign and mysterious work of regeneration is itself performed by truth: 'Being born again . . . by the word of God' [1 Peter 1:23]. For this reason Paul is repetitiously insistent that 'words easy to be understood' are a *sine qua non* of edification. It is possible to think upon truth without the Spirit's gracious influence; but we are never encouraged to expect to receive the Spirit's gracious influence without truth meeting the mind.

Remembering the Biblical stress upon intelligent communication of information for edification, what reason have we to believe that one who spoke in tongues was unaware of the mysteries spoken [v. 2]? If all others were dependent upon clear and intelligible truth for their edification, how could a man speaking in tongues even build up himself [v. 4] unless there was some dim intellectual perception of the mystery being spoken by his lips? Perhaps his grasp was not sufficient to interpret. Nevertheless there must be an intelligent comprehension on the part of the tongues-speaker if he is to benefit. If this conclusion is not valid, the responsibility to produce Biblical proof must rest with those of the contrary opinion.[2]

Those who say that to speak in tongues in private devotions is edifying must ask themselves a number of questions. Is there anything intelligible in the tongues-messages? Are the messages based upon an emotional experience that has bypassed the mind? If so, what Biblical warrant is there for such a form of worship? It is criticized even by 1 Cor. 14.

If 1 Cor. 14:1–19 urges anything, it is to keep central the most plain and intelligent form of truth. Today it must not even be prophecy but the

---

[2] To hold that tongues-speakers are ignorant of their revelations, one must answer Charles Hodge on 1 Cor. 14:14.

completely suited, face-to-face revelation which came by Jesus Christ. What could be more edifying than the clear notes [vv. 7, 8] of gospel exposition? The word of Christ plainly taught is the supreme height of spiritual edification to believers alive upon the earth.

One Purpose For Tongues

'Brethren, be not children in understanding: howbeit in malice be ye children, but in understanding be men. In the law it is written, With men of other tongues and other lips will I speak unto this people; and yet for all that will they not hear me, saith the Lord. Wherefore tongues are for a sign, not to them that believe, but to them that believe not: but prophesying serveth not for them that believe not, but for them which believe' [1 Cor. 14:20–22].

A mountain of Scripture has already buried 'tongues' under a heap of prohibition in 1975. But these verses hold another argument against their modern use. Already we have seen from Scripture that tongues were one of the signs of an apostle, accrediting him as an agent of divine revelation. While the childhood state of affairs continued, tongues also served temporarily to edify believers, partially and dimly. Yet the apostle wants believers fully informed about tongues. He urges in v. 20, 'In understanding be men'. Do not be like some charismatics who want to escape doctrinal discussions or close Bible study. Be men in understanding. Dig into the mine of the Old Testament.

Isaiah 28:11 and 12 are the verses that Paul quotes at this point. Foundation texts for tongues! Such words were spoken while the majority of God's prophets had been sent speaking Hebrew. All truth was delivered in their language. What a privilege! It was to continue so until the days of Jesus Christ. Suddenly at Pentecost the truth of God would be spoken in men's ears in Gentile languages. This was no promising sign to the Jewish nation; rather was it a sign of condemnation. Even with Galileans speaking in languages of the nations, Israel would not repent, but would display hardness of heart. 'For all that will they not hear me, saith the Lord.' Tongues were a sign to the Jews of impending doom, the destruction of 70 A.D.

A conclusion is reached at verse 22. Tongues are a sign to unbelievers, but not a sign which will convince them of unbelief to bring about conversion! Verse 23 shows that tongues will only make unbelievers think the gifted 'mad'. Tongues are a sign of God's displeasure and hastening wrath, especially upon his negligent firstborn, Israel.

Again we ask, what purpose could tongues serve today? The apostles are dead, so tongues-speaking cannot credit them with divine authority any longer. Face-to-face revelation has come, there is no need for dim, partial edification as children by tongues. Tongues never did signify spiritual depth and reality in the speaker. The Jews came under the hand of awful wrath long ago. The terrible collapse has taken place. If anything, we now look for blessing to return to Israel [Romans 11]. Tongues will not serve that purpose. Why should tongues continue today? They do not. They have ceased.

'And the spirits of the prophets are subject to the prophets.' [1 Cor. 14:32]. Some saints will read vv. 23–29 with a puzzled look. Being used to a 'hit or miss' fastening upon individual verses they will ask, 'Doesn't it say, "Covet to prophesy"? Haven't you read, "Forbid not to speak with tongues"? How then can you exclude these things today?' Anyone who has followed the apostle's argument to this point will at once see the fallacy of ignoring all the prior premises. Conclusions are simple in a syllogism without premises. So is the isolated text approach to tongues. Those unwilling to follow through all that is said must wander in darkness. We can only shout to them, 'I would not have you ignorant' [12:1]. If they will not bring their minds to think the problem through, they will wrest the Scriptures they cite.

There is one subsidiary point worth noting in verses 28–32. When the Holy Spirit came upon men in New Testament times, this never resulted in the loss of self-control. Again this is an implication of 12:1 & 2. When the spirit of tongues entered a man, he had the ability to think rationally about his situation, and he maintained the power to keep quiet. The spirits of the prophets were always subject to the prophets. The more careful and sober charismatics loathe wild and disorderly meetings where folks are 'out of control' and where confusion exists. God's Spirit always works in a way consistent with the use of man's intelligence and self-control.

Still, the chief aim of this chapter is not to distinguish between degrees of charismatic wisdom. 1 Cor. 12–14 demonstrates the indefensibility of the entire modern pentecostal movement in all its shades and forms. It denies that the miraculous is any indication of spiritual grace. It insists that revelatory gifts must cease when the Scriptures are complete.

6: WHY CHRISTIANS
SEEK 'THE GIFTS'

To-day's Appeal

Ignorant of the force of New Testament views on miraculous gifts, many true Christians have been attracted to the pentecostal company. Consequently they have been turned aside from the firm foundation of Scripture as sole authority for their lives. If this is not the case, then they are ignoring the prophecies which they claim have come from God. But this distrust of Holy Writ insinuates itself unconsciously into the believer's heart and life. Attention has been fixed on issues other than the unique authority and sufficiency of the Word. It is important to analyse the force of gravity which pulls God's people into the orbit of neo-pentecostalism. What is it that attracts sober disciples of Christ into the unbiblical beliefs and practices of neo-pentecostalism?

So rapid and so wide has been the spread of 'the charismatic' in the last fifteen years, that it is difficult to characterize the entire movement. Many who participate in 'miraculous gifts' refuse to be called Pentecostals or 'charismatics'. They have seen so many wild-fire abuses that they wish no association with the popular label. Their aim is to keep 'charismata' in a place subordinate to Bible study, holy living, communion with God, and evangelism. At the opposite extreme are the flagrantly immoral and heretical, who evidence the same 'charismata' in the name of Christianity. In between lie the masses of Pentecostals who have a well-defined doctrine of the baptism in the Spirit. There are also the neo-pentecostals of general evangelical allegiance and denominational affiliation, who may or may not agree with the pentecostal theory. And we cannot forget the churchless crowd that knows its only religion in a charismatic society or house fellowship. All are seeking for or exercising or sitting under the ministry of what they would call 'gifts of the Spirit' or 'miraculous manifestations of the Spirit.'

Though the mutations are infinite in number, the species is one. Its identifying marks are clear. All run dangerously counter to the New Testament doctrine of revelation, by claiming revelatory gifts to be in existence in modern times. A second common mark has been alluded to already, but will now hold our attention more fully. For it is this element which captivates the minds of believers who are drawn to the 'charismatic'. The second mark is a search for something more from God, this 'something more' being identified in some way with 'supernatural manifestations of the Spirit'. Most often the 'charismata' are mentally linked with a second work of grace, or with a momentary experience which supplies the 'something more' sought after.

Testimonies of charismatics glow with records of something more from God in connection with their 'miraculous' experiences. How wide is the the range of desires which these testimonies appeal to in the Christian! 'More of success', on a very low level. 'More of a holy walk', 'more of intimate communion with God', 'more of power to glorify the Lord effectively in service', at the high end of the scale. 'More love for men', 'more satisfaction with life', 'more warmth of personality', in between low and high. The list can grow and the combinations of what the 'more' holds are as varied as the testimonies, or at least as varied as the groups in which they are given. Usually there is something of greater spiritual depth, holiness and power, whether these are conceived of Biblically or otherwise.

Finally all the blessed desires are generally identified with the exercise of miraculous gifts. Most Pentecostals hold as an article of faith that 'speaking in tongues' is *the* initial sign of baptism in the Spirit, which experience brings a deeper life than mere conversion. *The* gift sought is the Spirit. All other miraculous gifts are possessed only by those who have climbed to this higher plane of Christianity, though manifestations other than tongues need not follow. Thus spiritual gifts are clearly associated with possessing more spiritually. Some neo-pentecostals would say that the possession of any of the gifts may initially signify entrance to the deeper spiritual standing. A very few would say that no miraculous gift is necessary as a sign of entering the fulness of blessing they advocate. Yet in their minds there is an admiration for the miracle-worker, a conviction that one who really manifests the Holy Spirit in 'doing wonders' must be a person very near to the Lord.

It is certainly this combination of thought which attracts outsiders to Pentecostalism and keeps those who have been converted under its ministry. There is 'something more' to be had spiritually, and 'miraculous gifts' evidence that the miracle worker has gotten it. His advice is then sought at public meeting or in private interview, which confirms the identity of spiritual gifts with spiritual man.

Need we return to the example of Judas, to Matthew 7:21-23, to 1 Cor. 13:1-3 to demolish this fallacy? Have we not concluded that spiritual gifts do not identify a spiritual man? Many miracle workers will be disowned by Christ in the judgment. Inward graces or fruits of the Spirit, not outward displays of gift, are the signs of spirituality. Why must this ignorant and erroneous opinion continue? Many without showing much of the fruit of the Spirit are performing what modern men accept as miracles. Others in the pentecostal movement are godly men. But it is not their 'charismatic gifts' which lead us to that conclusion. It is *solely* the marks of grace in their characters. Whether they speak with tongues or heal contributes nothing to our opinion. Amazing and spectacular 'charismata' were never given to identify their possessors as spiritual men. They were given as credentials to apostolic authority and as a temporary means of edifying the whole body of the church. They could not be an indication of deeper spiritual vitality.

Furthermore if the ear and eye were keenly alert to charismatic words and literature, great doubt would be cast on the whole thesis. In spite of phenomenal growth in numbers, Pentecostals are involved in as much confusion as are other branches of Christianity. Their sober and wise spiritual leaders call attention to the same appalling ignorance, immorality, coldness of heart and impotence within their ranks that many have sought to escape by their experiences. A few voices are calling for more concentration upon the inscripturated Word of God. That is far more to the point. If this second blessing and 'charismatic gifts' are shared by the weaklings in their midst, then the 'more' we seek must come by the Word and the Spirit, not by some identification with their gifts. Is their movement properly called a revival? Not at all!

Apart from the gifts themselves, what of another distinct experience which will lift a believer from one level of grace to another? After all, it is this strand of evangelical thinking which paved the way for Pentecostalism. All knowledgeable charismatics pay honourable respect to teachers of the Keswick or deeper-life movement.[3] Too often this movement has led directly to the attitude of seeking to return to a church like that of apostolic days and to the simplistic identity of spiritual gift with spiritual man. But how is the approach made?

Advocates of a second experience of grace invite our attention to their survey of today's church. They rightly point to her impotence in the face of the world and the flesh. Every true believer must admit that the twentieth-century church desperately needs heavenly assistance to resist the forces of paganism. God must be sought after if we are to regain the moral and spiritual

[3] Notice du Plessis' salute to Andrew Murray in *The Spirit Bade Me Go*, p. 55. Andrew Murray's search for *The Full Blessing of Pentecost* culminated in many of his students becoming Pentecostals. For fuller historic evidence of Pentecostalism's relationship to second-work-of-grace teachings, see *A Theology of the Holy Spirit* by Frederick Dale Brunner, Eerdmans, 1970. Chapter II of this book (Part One) convincingly shows the link. It is no secret among charismatics. They usually own it openly.

ground which has been lost in a depraved society.

A cure is then suggested for the church's ills. Her condition requires some super-Christians, men who live on a higher plane of sanctification, who are endued with dynamic force. In other ages the church has had extraordinary men – a Luther, a Whitefield, an Edwards. It is often implied that these revered figures of church history embraced the teaching which is being promoted. There is, however, no historic support for such assertions. Luther, Edwards, and other such heroes of the past never espoused a 'second-work-of-grace doctrine'.[4] Then optimistic reports of spiritual giants of this decade and of their feats are recounted in order to drive home the lesson that one need not struggle on in the weakness of only one work of grace.

How is the humble saint to react? There he is, wrestling with sin and moral weakness. His

---

[4] Not infrequently those who appeal to history quote some of the moving experiences of Christian leaders of the past and then explain those experiences by teaching which these leaders would have firmly denied. Whitefield, Edwards and others knew, at times, a mighty enduement of the Spirit for their work but, unlike John Wesley, they did not err in supposing that every Christian must seek a second and distinct work of the Spirit after his conversion. See Edwards' work *The Distinguishing Marks of a Work of the Spirit of God*. Though he witnessed great revivals he wrote strongly against any expectation of the church receiving the extraordinary gifts of the Spirit, e.g. in his *Charity and Its Fruits*, 315–320.

service to Christ seems so fruitless. He can only pant in his soul for such victory in sanctification and such success in bringing honour to his God as is set before him from the past and the present. When a way is offered to join the ranks of the mighty, the poor Christian leaps with his heart before his head can think of the issue of Biblical authority.

If ever the appeal for a second work of grace has tugged at your soul, you ought to study carefully the last four chapters of Second Corinthians. There Paul was addressing the patriarchs who begat Pentecostalism and every other second-work-of-grace movement. Much can be lost through poor habits of reading Scripture. It is common to read one chapter and to fix attention chiefly upon favourite verses – verses which the reader may have long interpreted apart from the context. Read 2 Corinthians, chapters 10–13 all at once. Make a definite effort to observe the unity of the passage and to grasp Paul's main argument.

Corinthian Appeal

The apostle to the Gentiles is addressing a party in the church of Corinth which questioned his apostolic authority. In 13:3 Paul notes, 'Ye seek a proof of Christ speaking in me.' They doubted the authority of the man who planted their church. With boldness they openly challenged him to prove his apostleship. It is clear that the proof they sought was a testimony to extraordinary experiences of visions and revelations. In 12:1 Paul reluctantly said in effect, 'I will come to the matter of visions and revelations; for that is what you are demanding.' The opposition party at Corinth was convinced that spectacular mystical experiences were signs of super-spiritual individuals. Only such persons would be able to lead the church on to victory, revival, and success. Remarkable prophets would be worthy teachers!

This opinion was fostered at Corinth by certain dynamic leaders who were 'transforming themselves into the apostles of Christ' [11:13]. But they really preached 'another Jesus'; they had 'another spirit'; they taught 'another gospel' [11:4]. Yet by their stunning performances they would 'commend themselves' [10:12 & 18].

New men were presenting themselves as hyper-apostles or higher-apostles. That is the literal meaning of the words translated 'chiefest apostles' in 11:5, 'For I suppose I was not a whit behind the very chiefest apostles'. In this text Paul is not comparing himself to Peter and James, but to the new super-apostles. His reference was to men who were parading visions, revelations, and dynamic mystical experiences before the church. They boasted themselves to be God's gift to the church. Since they were a superior breed of apostles, they offered to take the church on to higher ground.

Consequently the people at Corinth began to compare Paul to the great mystics (much as the average pastor today may be compared with spectacular miracle men).[5] The new leaders were impressive, dynamic ministers. Paul appeared as an almost comic figure when placed next to them. He had no magnetic personality, no commanding appearance, no reports of smashing success. His churches were small, struggling, and problem-ridden. His own life was constantly beset by trial and tragedy. They recalled that Paul was not eloquent. In 11:6 the apostle takes note of their opinion that he was 'rude in speech'. He brings their total evaluation into clear focus in 10:10: 'For his letters, say they, are weighty and powerful; but his bodily presence is weak, and his speech contemptible.'

No doubt there are some modern counterparts to the Corinthian super-apostles. Elements of their arrogance and showmanship are found in charismatic circles. However, this is not meant to suggest that all or even the majority of Pentecostals fit this aspect of the description. Nor are such displays of the flesh limited to neo-pentecostalism. They are sadly found in all wings of the modern church, especially in America. But the

[5] Cf. 10:12.

[70]

basic elements common throughout Pentecostalism are all here, though others might be far less crass in their presentation. There is 'something more' spiritually for the Corinthians. The higher life of true religion is associated with phenomenal 'gifts'. Paul's response will give some indication of his attitude toward second-work-of-grace ideas.

Biblical Response

A direct answer to this challenge, begins in 11:18: 'Seeing that many glory after the flesh, I will glory also.' Paul will boast as do the super-apostles. However as his boast begins there is a biting irony in his words which mocks his enemies' foolish pride. Any claim to having arrived on a higher plane of grace reflects an element of vainglory. However much one may wish to assist the unfortunate 'mere convert', there is an air of esteeming self better than others. This is true whether the new standing is a deeper life or a baptism in the Spirit. It is reflected in the argument that those who have not received the full blessing of the second work suffer church ills and personal failure because they have not taken the all-important second step. Whereas if a church has troubles and the believer's life reflects impotence, what is needed is revival of, or a fresh portion of the 'more' already possessed.

A paraphrase of the apostle's main argument in

11:23–33 could well be put in the following terms: 'I work hard, sweating, toiling, struggling. What has such labour accomplished? I have been beaten, imprisoned, nearly killed. I have been shipwrecked, stoned, robbed, conspired against. I have been tired, aching, hungry, thirsty, cold, naked. I am constantly concerned about the churches.' Verse 29 reaches the climax; he could well sympathize with the weakness of others: 'Who is weak and I am not weak?' It certainly does not appear to be a very forceful defence, addressed as it was to people who were already prepared to say, 'This apostle is a weakling'!

In verses 32 and 33 the final knife of ridicule is thrust into the sides of his boasting counterparts in Corinth. It is as if Paul were saying, 'I can picture the church in a fascinating testimony meeting. You have just been hearing the triumphant deeds of the super-apostles. There has been no lack of dreams, visions, miracles. The air is charged with expectations of hearing further reports of the astounding power of God. Well, here is my experience to read at your meeting. 'You may picture me as the little man that I am. There is Paul, frightened, and huddled in a basket. He was furtively lowered over the wall of Damascus, running for his life. The incident, which you well remember, is most characteristic of my life-experiences. That is how I deserve to be remembered. There you have the real Paul.'

In chapter 12 Paul continues his defence: 'I will come to visions and revelations' [v. 1]. It was the current fashion at Corinth. The people would hang on to the edges of their seats to hear of such things. But again there is cutting sarcasm. We may justly read between the lines of the first six verses of chapter 12 in this manner: 'I had an extraordinary revelation fourteen years ago. Your new apostles have them daily and parade new visions at every meeting. But I am afraid that I must go back in my memory fourteen years to recall a significant mystical experience involving revelations. I hope it does not disappoint your keen curiosity, but I must be very negative. I am not certain what state I was in. And I cannot tell you anything that I saw. (How that must injure your raging thirst for the sensational!) As a matter of fact I am going to change the subject quickly.'

Nevertheless there was a vital lesson for the church to be drawn from Paul's revelation experience. Verse 7 of chapter 12 teaches us that the apostle's surpassing revelation was followed by dreadful struggles with his own flesh and with Satan. A thorn in the flesh was given to Paul, a goad to stir up his remaining flesh. It was a messenger of the devil.

Far from transporting Paul to a plane of victory

and grand sanctification, extraordinary revelation signalled the start of a more desperate struggle against sin and the flesh. God had permitted his apostle to fall into this time of grievous temptation lest he become proud. After Paul witnessed the glories of the 'third heaven', God would make him vividly aware of the flesh which remained in his own bosom. It would prevent a haughty spirit in the Lord's servant.

Verse 8 reminds us how wretched was Paul's struggle after his extraordinary experience. He noted his temptation, and three times he assaulted the gates of heaven with determined petitions to have the cursed messenger of Satan taken from him. But it was not God's will. Was the revelation given to Paul a sign of special sanctification? No, the struggle with the flesh increased. Was Paul by his exotic experience a more forceful individual? To the contrary, more time had to be given to this personal battle against temptation. He saw more clearly his flesh and felt that he was weaker.

Verses 9–12 of chapter 12 emerge from the heavy atmosphere of irony into the clear air of stated principle. In these few verses the apostle hurls a dart which strikes at the advocate of all second-work-of-grace teachings. It is a straightforward and masterful handling of the issue. Verse 9 sounds the true spirit of the Christian:

'Most gladly therefore will I rather glory in my infirmities, that the power of Christ may rest upon me.'

Paul feels a deep satisfaction in calling attention to his personal weaknesses. He has already told us of his constant awareness of natural and moral weakness. He knows that he is a man in one desperate crisis after another. He feels a dreadful war with the flesh and the devil. But he delights in his infirmities because when something happens through his ministry, it is evident to all the world that it has happened by the power of Christ. His Lord will receive all the glory.

The apostle Paul lays no claim to being a superman. His readers should recall the spirit in which he had first come to Corinth. He had come to them with neither eloquence nor confidence, but he did know fear and trembling [1 Corinthians 2:1–4]. Yet sinners were converted and a church was begun. How could they explain it? Was the explanation that he was a mighty super-Christian who had taken a second step and reached a victorious plane of living? Paul knew that this would be an absurd suggestion to any who knew him personally. God's Spirit prospered his ministry for one reason – *it pleased God*. Certainly Paul possessed a remarkable intellect. Yet there were, no doubt, greater minds than his which never shook the world. It was God's grace attending the apostle's work which alone explains his effectiveness. He was still only a weak thing called to confound the mighty of the world. The lesson is that God's power is glorified in using weak Christians.

Certainly the modern church should long for and pray for revival. She should petition God for a wider spread of his truth. She should ask for a restoration of a generally higher level of righteousness in his people and in society at large. God's people should request that greater numbers be brought to know his gracious salvation. Nevertheless they must realize that there is no necessity of having men of super-sanctification as a means to revival.

God uses rather ordinary Christians who are engaged in a desperate struggle against their own flesh and against the devil to magnify his greatness in revival. Instruments greatly used of God must be actively fighting temptation and praying for the removal of sin from their hearts, even as Paul cried to God against his thorn in the flesh. But the apostle is showing that God does greatly use men who yet have personal problems in wrestling with sin. And our mighty Lord receives more glory because it is evident that the power has come sovereignly from him.

Super-sanctified Christians would be lacking in a major qualification which God requires of his

servants, namely, a deep sense of personal un-
worthiness and uncleanness. Without a very low
evaluation of himself, the servant of Christ cannot
be meek in approaching sinners. Nor can he
heartily give all praise to God for all success
granted to him.

In Luke 5 Peter saw the fish miraculously
brought to his net by our Lord. At that moment
'he fell down at Jesus' knees, saying, Depart
from me: for I am a sinful man, O Lord.' He knew
that he was unworthy to stand in the presence of
the Saviour; he was too unclean to be associated
with him. Our Master immediately responded,
'Fear not, from henceforth thou shalt catch men.'
It is as if Christ had said, 'Now that you are fully
aware of your moral impurity, you are prepared
to serve me, Simon.'

When prophets of the Old Testament were
called to a mighty work, their calls usually began
with a conscious awareness of their personal
impurity and impotence. Just so, God would
rather keep Paul buffeted with some Satanic
temptation stirring up his flesh, than allow his
servant to think himself exalted above others. The
greatness of Paul's work came by the measure of
God's mighty Spirit attending his ministry, not
through the moral excellence of the instrument
God used.

In our Biblical desire for revival, we must

refuse to seek any experience which proposes to eliminate our natural weakness. God did not spread the gospel of Christ through the world by means of extrovert personalities. Christ did not choose apostles for their native strength of character. The church was not begun by twelve emperors but by twelve political slaves of Rome. Our Lord had no special use for scholars. Most of the apostles were far from learned. His choice of evangelists included no warriors, nor 'Madison Avenue' publicity men. As a group, the apostles had no outstanding personal strength which can explain their impact on the world.

In various ways Christians reveal their suspicion that only extraordinary men can be used for great works of God. Some place a great emphasis on academic skills. They think, 'If we send men with respected academic honours through the world, the nations will recognize genius and come to Christ.' Others advertise football players, theatre stars, and politicians, expecting that the world will run to their meetings. Unfortunately, though the crowds come they are not changed. Why should they not remain worldly after this appeal to human greatness?

At times we may say too much of Whitefield's eloquence and Edwards' scholarship. We sometimes romanticize the lives of leaders in revivals. John Knox, so remarkably used in the Reformation of the 16th Century, declared before his death, 'In youth, mid-age, and now after many battles, I find nothing in me but vanity and corruption'. Such was Whitefield's sense of personal unfitness that he said he could not enter a pulpit but for the imputed righteousness of Christ. The last words of that burning light, William Grimshaw of Yorkshire, were, 'Here goes an unprofitable servant'. It was grace which made these Christians what they were, and had it not been for the Spirit of God attending their ministries they would have remained as obscure as many another who was equal to them in natural ability.

Some of the most profound acts of witnessing and successful evangelism have been performed by the most unlikely, and unprepossessing individuals. Great numbers believed on Christ through the immoral Samaritan woman on the day she first met the Saviour. God did not wait until she had established a super-holy reputation among them. The blind man of John 9 was called upon to witness before the greatest Bible scholars in the world during the week of his conversion. God did not need someone who had mastered sound doctrine. The young believer bore a fine testimony.

God does not need your talents, wisdom, holiness, and strength. But rather you, in weakness, desperately need the power of his Spirit in your labours. You need not be wonderfully transformed by a second work of grace to be a suitable instrument of God's Spirit. The Lord delights in exalting his gracious power by using weak instruments.

Revival depends upon the sovereign blessing of God. Why should you be taken in by gimmicks? Why should you be turned aside by talk of a second work of grace? It is diverting attention from the penitent waiting upon God which should mark today's church. God revives his church through humble people who have real flaws, but who rely upon his grace alone as they diligently labour according to his Word. Of course we are all incompetent to be used by God in any work. We always will be. 'Who is sufficient for these things?' [2 Corinthians 2:16]. No one! It is foolish to labour for sufficiency to serve God. If it were achieved, one would need no continuing grace. Rather note that at every moment his grace is sufficient for thee as it was for Paul [2 Corinthians 12:9]. You will be in desperate need of grace throughout your life. In the midst of conscious weakness, rely on the grace of God. Spirituality must not be equated with personal power. Being weak is not to be construed as being carnal.

Pentecostalism is diverting men from admitting their weakness and relying on God's grace as sufficient. It has rather prompted men to seek personal sufficiency. As we have seen in earlier chapters, neo-pentecostals direct men away from truth to achieve sufficiency. The unique authority of the Scripture is undermined in the process. Experience is offered which is realized apart from the divinely appointed means of truth.

7: BAPTISM WITH
THE SPIRIT

'Full gospel' forces have influenced Christians by addressing themselves to inward longings which always will attend the saints on earth. In their offer of immediate entrance upon a new plane of spirituality, Pentecostals have used a Biblical phrase which has made their solution seem credible. 'Baptism with the Spirit' is proposed as a second experience to be sought by believers.

Hungry Christians are often strangers to sound Biblical instruction on this subject. Recent 'charismatic' interpretation of the phrase is the only explanation ever to reach their ears. When truth is silent, false views seem plausible. Therefore it is necessary to understand something of the Scriptural meaning of the popular phrase.

'Baptize with the Holy Ghost' are words used on only three historic occasions in the Bible. All four Gospels record John the Baptist's testimony to Christ in much the same way as Mark 1:8: 'I indeed have baptized you with water: but he shall baptize you with the Holy Ghost.' Then on the last occasion that our Lord talked with his disciples, on the day of his ascension, he said, 'For John truly baptized with water; but ye shall be baptized with the Holy Ghost not many days hence.' [Acts 1:5]. Finally, in Acts 11:16, Peter used the following words to describe his reaction to events at Cornelius' house, 'Then remembered I the word of the Lord, how that he said, John indeed baptized with water; but ye shall be baptized with the Holy Ghost.' By examining Acts 1 and 2 we can see the fulfilment of the prophecy of John and Jesus.

Acts 1:4-5 uses the phrases 'The promise of the Father' and 'baptized with the Holy Ghost' to identify one and the same blessing. The disciples were to wait in Jerusalem for the promise of the Father. Then Jesus reminds them of John's contrast as containing the promise they are to expect. It is important to recognize this identity of reference for these two phrases as we observe the fulfilment of both in chapter two.

In Acts 2:1-4 we read an account of the disciples being 'filled with the Holy Ghost'. There was a sound from heaven like a rushing, mighty wind. Cloven tongues as of fire visibly appeared and rested upon each one of them. They spoke with tongues. When objections were made to the strange behaviour of the disciples, Peter rose to explain the dramatic and unique incident of history and to apply its lesson to the crowds which had gathered.

At once Peter called attention to a promise of the Father by his prophet Joel [Joel 2:28-32]. In the last days the Spirit would be poured out upon

God's servants. When this occurred, his servants would prophesy. Notice again the clear Scriptural teaching that those who spoke in tongues on the day of Pentecost were prophesying. That was Peter's explanation of their speaking in tongues [Acts 2:15–18]. More central to our present discussion however is Peter's recognition of the day's events as the fulfilment of the Father's promise.

Peter's sermon did not turn to another topic when he began to speak of Jesus of Nazareth in verse 22. The apostle by divine inspiration was preaching the death, resurrection, and enthronement of Jesus Christ as the necessary preparation for the giving of the Holy Spirit. Verse 33 connects 'baptism with the Spirit' directly to the exaltation of our Lord. 'Therefore being by the right hand of God exalted, and having received of the Father the promise of the Holy Ghost, he hath shed forth this, which ye now see and hear.'

The work of the Spirit is not something in addition to the work of Christ. There is no separation between the saving work of God's Son and the sanctifying, empowering work of God's Spirit. Christ's atoning work secured the promise of the Spirit, and part of Christ's reigning work is to dispense the Spirit to his church. Men can be baptized with the Holy Ghost only after the enthronement of the risen Messiah. As John 7:39

teaches, the Son must be glorified for the Spirit to be given. As his first act of state, the newly-crowned Ruler of the universe poured out his Spirit upon the church. This is the significance of Pentecost.

When the hearts of Peter's audience were smitten with alarm, the apostle said: 'Repent, and be baptized every one of you in the name of Jesus Christ for the remission of sins, and ye shall receive the gift of the Holy Ghost. For the promise is unto you, and to your children, and to all that are afar off, even as many as the Lord our God shall call.' The 'gift of the Holy Ghost' could mean only the filling with the Spirit mentioned in verse 4. Their whole attention had been riveted on those who were baptized with the Spirit. Peter's whole sermon explained the experience of the disciples who had captured the crowd's attention. To offer them now another gift of the Spirit without a clear distinction would be the height of deception.

Verse 39 speaks of a promise. What promise could Peter mean? Their thoughts had been directed to only one promise for some time. It was the promise of the Holy Ghost cited in verse 33, explained by Joel 2:28–32. It was the very same promise to which Christ had called Peter's attention in 1:4 and for which Peter had waited at Jerusalem! To introduce some second and lesser promise, now that their souls were in distress for their sin of crucifying the Son of God, would have been the lowest form of opportunism. There is but one promise of the Father and one gift of the Holy Ghost throughout Acts 1 and 2.

Now, who was to receive this promise of the Father? What was required of them to be 'baptized with the Spirit'? Verse 39 quite clearly answers the first question and verse 38 the second. The promise discussed throughout Acts 1 and 2 was not made to an élite corps of extraordinary believers, but to 'as many as the Lord our God shall call'. The promise was not reserved for a more advanced breed of Christians. It applies to all who were and are effectually called into saving union with the exalted Christ.

Every convert shall be baptized with the Holy Ghost. After Pentecost there is no second-stage experience, no requirement beyond conversion, demanded as a condition for receiving the gift of the Holy Ghost. There is nothing of waiting, preparing or experiencing a second work of grace. It is simply, 'Repent, and be baptized . . . and ye *shall* receive the gift of the Holy Ghost.' John 7:39 indicates that after Christ was glorified, the Spirit (which flows from men in rivers for abundance) was to be given to them 'that believe'. No qualification beyond simple, saving faith is suggested.

When Peter observed the Spirit fall on the household of Cornelius, it signified to him that 'God hath also to the Gentiles granted repentance unto life' [Acts 11:18]. His logic was, 'The promise belonged to converts. They have received the promise. Therefore they must be converts'. It was a radical conclusion for a Jew. But the logic was compelling. Jesus had baptized them with his Spirit; therefore Peter must baptize them with water in the name of Christ, though they were not circumcised. Again our main interest is in the coincidence of conversion and baptism with the Spirit.

In every Bible passage which mentions Jesus baptizing with the Holy Ghost, there is a contrast with John's water baptism. John was the last prophet of the old covenant. Jesus baptized with the Spirit as the new covenant Prophet. Old Testament Scriptures had predicted that baptism with the Spirit would be a distinctive blessing of the new covenant. Baptism with the Spirit then must bring to every member of Christ's church all of the blessings comprehended in the essential distinction between old covenant blessings and new covenant experience.

The Spirit poured forth by the exalted Saviour has brought all believers to a higher plane of spiritual life and understanding than that which was experienced by Old Testament saints. Of this we are told in Jeremiah 31:31–34 and Hebrews 8:10–13. Baptism with the Spirit certainly involves a greater cleansing of the heart, a writing of God's law upon the heart, and the abiding of the Spirit in believers as foretold in Ezekiel 36:22–27.

The contrast is not absolute; for the Spirit was present and working in the lives of believers before Pentecost. As Jesus declared before his death, in John 14:17, the Spirit already dwelt with his disciples. But there is a decided contrast. Because of Christ's exaltation there is a fulness of blessing, an effusion of the Spirit, and a presence of the Spirit unknown in times past. Since Pentecost, all of God's promises in the covenant of grace have come to fuller realization in men's hearts by the Spirit.

As the Book of Acts begins to describe the effects of the Spirit being poured out, the focus of attention is upon the spiritual quality of life in the church [see 2:41–47]. Luke notes the love for the apostles' doctrine, and fellowship at the Lord's table and in prayer. He shows transformed lives. There is the opening of hearts and pocketbooks to needy brethren, and a singleness of heart in the assembly. Then God's grace in his Spirit is manifested in daily additions to the church. At the same time Luke records, 'many wonders and signs were done by the apostles' [verse 43] – not by

[88]

all saints, but by the authoritative spokesmen of God's Word.

All blessings are the direct results of an active ministry of Christ carried out upon his throne. His church has been introduced to increased knowledge, grace, and spirituality by his sending of the Holy Spirit. Had Jesus not told his apostles to expect greater works from believers than he had done himself? In foretelling the Spirit's coming [John 14:12] he had solemnly predicted, 'He that believeth on me, the works that I do shall he do also; and greater works than these shall he do; because I go unto my Father.'

Pentecostals have suggested that the same works and the greater works must refer to miracles. If so the prophecy has fallen to the ground unfulfilled. We have no reason to believe that any apostle performed miraculous works equal to those of the Son of God. Nor do modern reports of wonders begin to savour of Christ's greatness. We know of nothing which even approximates to changing water into wine, to feeding 5,000 with a few barley loaves, or to raising from the dead one who has been in the grave four days. We know of none who can read the innermost secrets of the heart and answer unasked questions. Jesus' miracles stand in a category by themselves.

But the exalted Christ by pouring out his

Spirit has done 'greater works' through his servants than were seen during his earthly life. The apostles themselves experienced a deeper spiritual transformation after our Lord ascended. It was expedient for them that he go away. Their spiritual depth in Acts 2 is profoundly greater than during Christ's lifetime. Though they had healed the sick and cast out devils while Jesus was on earth, they never preached and counselled the church as they did after receiving the Spirit. No work of Jesus while he was upon earth brought 3,000 souls to spiritual birth by one sermon. After all has been said, is not the radical change of a soul and the rescue of a man from everlasting torment greater than the babbling of voices and restoration of bodily health?

Alas, Pentecostals have diverted our attention from the greater things to the lesser! Evangelical leaders of the past made no such mistake. Martin Luther, for example, commenting on 'the greater works' to be performed by believers according to John 14:12, writes:

'But which works of the Christian accomplish this? We see nothing special that they do beyond what others do, especially since the day of miracles is past. Miracles, of course, are still the least significant works, since they are only physical and are performed for only a few people. But let us consider the true, great works of which Christ speaks here – works which are done with the power of God, which accomplish everything, which are still performed and must be performed daily as long as the world stands. Christians have the Gospel . . . by means of which they convert people, snatch souls from the clutches of the devil, wrest them from hell and death, and bring them to heaven.'[1]

Likewise we find C. H. Spurgeon preaching as follows: 'He sent them forth', he says, referring to Christ's commission to the disciples, *'to work miracles* as well as to preach. Now, he hath not given us this power, neither do we desire it: it is more to God's glory that the world should be conquered by the force of truth than by the blaze of miracles. The miracles were the great bell of the universe which was rung in order to call the attention of all men all over the world to the fact that the gospel feast was spread: we do not need the bell now . . . For the moral and spiritual forces of truth to work by themselves, apart from any physical manifestation, is more to the glory of the truth, and the Christ of the truth, than if we were all miracle workers, and could destroy gainsayers. Yet still, though we work no miracles in the physical world, we work them in the moral and spiritual world.'[2]

[1] Luther's *Works*, vol. 24, 79 (Concordia Publishing House).
[2] *The Metropolitan Tabernacle Pulpit*, vol. 23, 471.

In our generation there are those who have waited long for God to bare his right arm of power. The church looks to the exalted Jesus to dispense a greater measure of his Spirit in our day. But the 'full gospel' teaching has turned many aside from waiting on the Lord for true revival. They have adjusted the hopes of the church to the possession of outward gifts. Men have begun to look upon the healing of bodies as a mark of God's gracious presence, and upon 'stammering lips and another tongue' as an answer to our prayers. Men are wanting to put the lesser works in the place of the greater.

May God grant his true servants grace to await life-revolutionizing conversion power as their desired goal! May churches pray till the earth is swept with powerful preaching of the Word that searches men, breaks hard hearts, and carries with it the Spirit of regeneration, repentance, and faith! Let us petition the sovereign throne of our holy Lord until we receive from him those most magnificent works of the Spirit – the bowing of hearts to his lordship, the renovation of character, and that turning of the world upside down which savours of the abundant fruits of the Spirit!

But as we petition the Lord, we cannot adopt the views of neo-pentecostals. Scripture insists that we view all genuine converts as having received the gift of the Father. Upon saving faith and repentance, all receive 'the baptism of the Holy Ghost'. The remarkable ministry of the Spirit, indicated by this phrase, is shared by all saints. It indicates an advance beyond old covenant experience. But it is not a second blessing reserved for a special band of Christians.

Experiences offered in 'charismatic' activities are extra-Biblical. They bear no resemblance to the 'baptism with the Spirit' promised in Scripture. God issues no call to re-enact the unique historic event of Pentecost. Only those who passed from old covenant to new covenant times could witness the dramatic beginning of the Spirit's work in the church. Now the Lord offers the gift of the Spirit to all who repent and are baptized for the remission of sins.

In its basic approach, the pentecostal doctrine of the baptism in the Spirit makes a fatal error common to all second-work-of-grace theories. First the attention of the believer is riveted upon every defective feature in his life. Then the conclusion reached is, 'You have not gone nearly far enough. You may have eternal life. But that is attended with meagre power, minimal holiness, unsatisfying communion with God. Unless you have a second experience you are doomed to a grim life'. What has this teaching done for the convert? It has shamefully degraded the work of the Saviour and the Spirit in his salvation.

Effectual calling, regeneration, justification, adoption and definitive sanctification have been made to appear most inadequate. Certainly this is unbiblical!

Perhaps it has all come about from the wretched habit of counting men as converts to Christ when they have merely gone through a mental exercise about basic gospel facts. With no evidences of regenerating grace or fruits of initial sanctification, worldly men have been pronounced 'Christian'. No wonder this sort of experience must then be debased in the eyes of the 'convert'! Indeed aspersions should be cast on his barren profession. He certainly needs to take another step — *the first* of repentance and faith.

But when the Bible addresses those who have the root of the matter in them, there is never a diminishing of the value of their experience. Honest self-examination is urged so that a believer may intelligently press forward in grace. Note the exhortation of 2 Pet. 1:5–11: 'And besides this, giving all diligence, add to your faith virtue; and to virtue, knowledge . . . Wherefore the rather, brethren, give diligence to make your calling and election sure: for if ye do these things, ye shall never fall: for so an entrance shall be ministered unto you abundantly into the everlasting kingdom of our Lord and Saviour Jesus Christ.' However, this effort is required, not because the child of God is lacking in some basic step of grace; it is the logical conclusion of asserting that he has already the necessary work of grace done in him if he is a child of God. Peter writes: 'According as his divine power hath given unto us all things that pertain unto life and godliness, through the knowledge of him that hath called us to glory and virtue: whereby are given unto us exceeding great and precious promises; that by these ye might be partakers of the divine nature, having escaped the corruption that is in the world through lust.'

Again, Romans 6 does not decry the believer's inadequate experience at conversion. Rather the chapter asserts what the Spirit has already done in him, namely, a great and magnificent work of sanctification and deliverance. Reckoning upon this then, the believer must press on in a lifelong battle with sin. And he must be victorious. Second-work-of-grace theories simply do not fit the Biblical data on a man's conversion which brings with it the baptism with the Spirit.

8: WHEN THE
SPIRIT COMES

Close investigation is demanded when anyone attributes his actions and teachings to the presence of God's Spirit. Scripture gives us a solemn warning when it commands, 'Beloved, believe not every spirit, but try the spirits whether they are of God: because many false prophets are gone out into the world' [1 John 4:1]. Since 'charismatic' groups profess that their amazing influence is the result of God's Spirit moving in their midst, they are inviting scrutiny. Application of a few tests to exciting movements of today would deliver many Christians from sorrow. Had they only known how to discern the ways of the Spirit, many never would have been burned by 'wild fire'.

God's Word provides the tests by which we are to judge the spirits. Psalm 85 is one passage which outlines for us definite marks which will be found in any revival produced by God the Holy Spirit. The first seven verses are a prayer for revival, including the plea, 'Wilt thou not revive us again; that thy people may rejoice in thee?' [v. 6]. Then there follows a description of expected blessings when revival does come [verses 8–13]. Two pertinent tests may be drawn from verse 11, 'Truth shall spring out of the earth; and righteousness shall look down from heaven.'

The Spirit of Holiness

One crucial gauge of true revival is holiness. 'Righteousness shall look down from heaven' [v. 11b]. Later the psalmist adds, 'Righteousness shall go before him (the Lord); and shall set us in the way of his steps' [v. 13]. We should expect holiness to mark all the work of God's Spirit, for the most prominent name of the third Person of the Godhead is '*Holy* Spirit'. The Spirit is infinitely, eternally, and unchangeably glorious in holiness. It is primarily because of his personal holiness that the adjective is so constantly used in his name; and the Spirit's being is so filled with purity that all his works shine with holiness.

In his work of creation the Spirit obviously laboured to form a holy world. When his work was completed, the Father pronounced it 'very good' [Genesis 1:31]. And in his redemptive work, God the Spirit joins the Father and the Son in giving his primary attention to making men holy. The Father chose 'us in him (Christ) before the foundation of the world, *that we should be holy and without blame before him*' [Eph. 1:4]. The Son 'hath reconciled (you) in the body of his flesh through death, *to present you holy and unblameable and unreproveable in his sight*' [Colossians 1:21, 22]. Just so the Spirit comes upon men to make them holy. When God promised the Spirit in Ezekiel 36:27 he said, 'I will put my spirit within you, and (thereby) *cause you to walk in my statutes, and ye shall keep my judgments and do them.*' It is his great aim to write the holy law of God upon the hearts of men.

Therefore when the Spirit comes upon any group of men, he will turn their attention chiefly to the issue of holiness. It is a mark of sin for men to be more concerned with their happiness than with their holiness. It is a mark of grace to seek personal righteousness above personal comfort. The Spirit is indeed a Comforter, bringing a sense of peace with God. Yet this peace comes in the wake of concern over holiness, and follows a disturbing sense of enmity against God.

A number of Pentecostals are deeply concerned about practical godliness. Yet they themselves are increasingly forced to complain that large segments of neo-pentecostalism show no concern for holy living.[1] If those who were seeking more from the Lord would objectively search neo-pentecostal groups for signs of Biblical holiness, large numbers of 'full-gospel' fellowships would be quickly shunned. Those who hunger and thirst after righteousness would find no appeal in the overwhelming attention given to happiness in

[1] See W. T. H. Richards, *Charismatic Movement in the Historic Churches*, in which he expresses his own concern and quotes other Pentecostals alarmed at rapidly growing numbers who participate in the 'gifts' but evidence no sanctification, pp. 12–15, Evangel Press, London, 1972.

many of these circles. But one must look beyond the 'miraculous gifts' to judge rightly.

Increasingly there are fellowships of 'charismatics' dominated by talk of personal satisfaction, joy, thrills and excitement. In this atmosphere concern for holiness evaporates. Even those who were originally attracted to Pentecostalism out of an aching desire to please the Lord with a more holy life turn aside to the selfish desire to please themselves with ever fresh spine-tingling encounters. Many fellowships where 'charismata' are quite abundant bear no resemblance whatever to the sobriety evident in Spirit-filled men pursuing righteousness.

When the Holy Spirit comes to sinful men, he initially brings sorrow. But in circles described above, there is only the boast of rapid transport to joy and peace. Any religious experiences which bring immediate rejoicing and uninterrupted cheerfulness are not to be trusted. There is much more to spirituality than a lifting of the spirits, an entering into the exuberant life, and an extending one's succession of thrilling experiences. Yet in many of the popular neo-pentecostal societies you will look in vain for anything else. Profoundly aware of this very perversion, some who are very familiar with charismatic trends have withdrawn from the fellowship and refuse to identify themselves with it.

But the Holy Spirit produces mourning for sin as he brings peace with God. He is not the 'Jolly Spirit' but the Holy Spirit. When the Spirit of Christ writes God's law upon the human heart, the person upon whom he has come is broken-hearted over past contempt for the law that he now loves. Memories of evil deeds which were once casually ignored become a distress to the conscience. Present inability to keep the spiritual law of God provokes grief. Scripture frequently joins sorrow for sin with the coming of the Spirit. It is a necessary ingredient of concern for personal holiness.

In Ezekiel 36:31 God tells his people what to expect when he puts his Spirit within them: 'Then shall ye remember your own evil ways, and your doings that were not good, and shall loathe yourselves in your own sight for your iniquities and for your abominations.' Again, in Zechariah 12:10 we have a promise of the pouring out the Spirit. At the time of fulfilment God tells us to look for men who 'mourn' and who 'shall be in bitterness.' Jesus told his disciples that when the Spirit came he would 'reprove (convince) the world of sin' [John 16:8]. When the Spirit came on the day of Pentecost thousands 'were pricked in their heart' and cried out in distress.

Not only does the Spirit bring an initial sorrow for sin, but he quickens a continuing sorrow for personal and national sin. The people of Christ are designated 'they that mourn' [Matthew 5:4]. Mixed with their heavenly joy is the sad parallel to Paul's experience in Romans 7. They struggle desperately against sin, for holiness is now their great aim.

We live in a culture which evidences the present wrath of God upon society. The general sexual immorality of our times is a certain sign that God in anger has given up the Western world to her lusts [Romans 1:18–25]. God has removed restraints from the naturally wicked hearts of Western men. Consequently the filthy abuses of men multiply. Such a flood of ungodliness is poured out in our civilization that none can escape the constant awareness of our culture's depravity.

No one who has God's Spirit can walk through our world without deep groanings of sorrow and distress. When the stench of immorality fills his nostrils, the Spirit-filled man cannot be happy, happy, happy all the day. As Christ wept for Jerusalem, his Spirit will cause tears to flow from us for our corrupt nation. If the Spirit were to come powerfully in the '70's it would not be to make men clap their hands for joy but to make them smite their breasts in sorrow. Lamentations would fill our streets as they filled Nineveh in Jonah's day. Surely there would be joy in personal deliverance from sin and prospects of heaven. Yet the spiritual man with a heart longing after holiness will vex his righteous soul from day to day in our modern Sodom. An absence of this disgust and sorrow with the pleasure-mad Western world indicates that the Spirit is yet to come in revival measure.

Sorrow for sin is an absent note in that portion of the charismatic movement that concentrates on the gifts to the neglect of holiness. 'Thrills', 'joy', 'gladness', 'happiness', 'satisfaction', 'peace', 'contentment', 'exciting experience' is the vocabulary of neo-pentecostalism. Some even cheapen the coming of the Spirit by likening it to having a good 'trip' on drugs. 'Turning on with Jesus' in a lighthearted experience is not a Spirit-given option to the necessary experience of his conviction for one's sin.

It cannot be said that all who are entering 'charismatic' ranks are doing so with a desire to know God and advance in purity of life. The 'more' from God that many are seeking is freedom from earthly troubles. Where 'the gifts' themselves hold primary attention, it is suggested that the Spirit will cure all ills and smooth all the rough bumps along the road of life. Nowhere is this so evident as in the popular emphasis on healing. The impression given by the 'full gospel' to the average believer is that God does not want his people to suffer in this world. If only Christians will believe, Spirit-filled men will heal them of anything. Sufferings are pictured as detrimental and undesirable for the Christian. Here is the candy-coated life, guaranteed to extract all bitter tastes.

Hebrews 12 has another view of suffering [vv. 1–11]. Sufferings in this life are appointed by God for the ultimate welfare of his people. The apostle does not suggest that more faith would guarantee escape from trials. Instead he counsels the patient endurance of afflictions. For all troubles are to be considered as chastenings of a loving heavenly Father who is doing us good. Sickness and trouble may be painful, but they are also profitable.

Hebrews 12 also indicates the Spirit-given attitude that is necessary if a person is to be patient under difficult providences from God's hand. A man must be serious about 'striving against sin' [v. 4]. The great motive held before Christians to make them patient is the future expectation of holiness. Verse 10 informs the church that God's chastenings are 'for our profit, that we might be partakers of his holiness'. God's Spirit gives men in whom he dwells so much hunger and thirst for righteousness that they are willing to endure sickness and other discomforts now. Spiritual men bear with these by fixing their eyes on the goal of

[103]

purifying the inward man. If God's method of sanctification is a rod, they will patiently submit. And it is clear to the Christian that suffering *is* one means by which the Almighty purges his purchased people. Mature believers confess with David, 'It is good for me that I have been afflicted' [Psalm 119:71].

As C. H. Spurgeon remarked, 'The greatest earthly blessing that God can give to any of us is health, *with the exception of sickness*. Sickness has frequently been of more use to the saints of God than health has. If some men, that I know of, could only be favoured with a month of rheumatism, it would, by God's grace, mellow them marvellously . . . I would not wish for any man a long time of sickness and pain; but a twist now and then one might almost ask for him. A sick wife, a newly-made grave, poverty, slander, sinking of spirit, might teach lessons nowhere else to be learned so well. Trials drive us to the realities of religion . . . our afflictions come to us as blessings, though they frown like curses.'[2]

When the Spirit comes in power he transforms a man's priority of interest. He subdues carnal selfishness which craves personal comfort and pleasure above all else. He implants a zeal for holiness which is willing to endure pain and sadness if it yields the fruit of righteousness. As

[2] *An All-Round Ministry*, Banner of Truth, pages 384, 385.

the Triune God aims first at the holiness of man and only subsequently at his happiness, so the redeemed man will aim pre-eminently at holiness.

In this distinguishing trait, considerable sections of the 'charismatic movement' are sadly lacking. While many talk of 'blowing their minds' on Jesus, and of 'exploding' in experiences of the Spirit, and finding happiness, we have heard too little of a sober interest in holiness. There is little of Spirit-induced sorrow for sin. There is little exposition and application of the blessed law of God. To very many 'full gospel' folk, holiness is an abstract, theoretical possession to be secured in one experience, then to be forgotten in the daily search for joy. Since this branch of Pentecostalism shares as much claim to 'miraculous gifts' and sudden experiences as do the sober and godly Pentecostals, the searcher for God must look for holiness of life and fruits of the Spirit, not for 'signs and wonders'.

The Spirit of Truth

A second mark of the reviving work of the Spirit, found in Psalm 85, is the flourishing of truth. 'Truth shall spring out of the earth' (verse 11). In this we are given a second rule for measuring the Spirit's presence. When the Holy Ghost is with men, attention will be given to doctrine. Men's minds will be captivated with truth. Our

Lord referred to the Holy Ghost as 'The Spirit of truth' [John 14:17, 15:26; 16:13]. It was he who moved men to write the Holy Scriptures [2 Peter 1:21]. He will never lead men to devalue the Bible nor to snub its doctrines. After the Spirit broke many hearts on the day of Pentecost with a conviction of sin, he moved the same men to continue 'steadfastly in the apostles' doctrine' [Acts 2:42]. The great first outpouring of the Spirit after Jesus' exaltation produced a profound love of the truth. The church's vitality came by way of her attention to doctrine.

Again, Pentecostal leaders will be found who are keenly determined that all God's counsel should be taught to their churches and friends. Once more they are compelled to deplore the ignorance of God's Word that is particularly obvious in the multiplying neo-pentecostal communions.[3] Wiser Pentecostals have become aware that whole churches and societies and meetings in the stream of neo-pentecostalism have increasingly scorned doctrine. A person who wishes to discuss Bible truth can scarcely find an interested ear in experience-centred 'charismatic' fellowships.

In neo-pentecostalism, the common experience of gifts has made it possible for men from

[3] See W. T. H. Richards, *op. cit.*, pp. 16–17, 29–30. Notice especially the quote from one alarmed leader, 'Teaching is more important than tongues'.

churches holding contrary teachings to fellowship in 'harmony'. 'Full gospel' societies embrace nuns and priests who continue to believe unbiblical doctrines. Some pentecostal Catholics have been so bold as to confess that their experiences of speaking in tongues have given them a deeper appreciation of the spiritual blessings of the mass, or have given them new dimensions of adoration for the 'blessed mother of our Lord'. The Spirit of truth will never move lips to utter such blasphemy and heresy. Neither will the Spirit of Christ silence his servants in the name of love and unity while soul-destroying doctrine is being taught.

Such silence in the face of heresy must be laid at the door of main-stream neo-pentecostals. The attitude of David du Plessis is positively irresponsible at this point. His tolerance of modernism, and his silence in respect of error on the foundation truths of the faith, are repeatedly apparent. His attitude cannot be explained as patience with new acquaintances while awaiting an opportunity to speak to them on basic matters. For when the opportunity comes to speak, he urges the newly-interested ones to receive the baptism with the Spirit without any inquiry as to whether they believe foundation truths. It is shocking to read of his satisfaction with the following situation: 'The most remarkable thing is that this [charismatic] revival is found in the so-called liberal societies and much less in the evangelical, and not at all in the fundamentalist segments of Protestantism. The last-mentioned are the most vehement opponents of this glorious revival because it is in the pentecostal movement and in the modernist World Council movements that we find the most powerful manifestations of the Spirit. This seems to be true almost without exception in most parts of the world, as far as I know.'[4]

The preservation of pure doctrine is of small account to many of the 'charismatic' people. Their experience of 'the Spirit' has ushered in a bond of unity irrespective of doctrine. Modernists who have dreamed of ecumenical union have openly greeted the pentecostal experiences as the key for unlocking the issues of faith and order which have kept the ecumenical door shut. And well they might greet the 'charismatic' phenomena. They have convinced even evangelicals to accept any who share remarkable 'experiences', regardless of the doctrine professed.

In the religious world it is modern Pentecostalism that has popularized philosophic existentialism which by-passes truth, or rather encounters 'truth' but with no possible objective communication of it. It is no wonder that neo-

[4] *The Spirit Bade Me Go*, p. 28.

orthodox theologians share charismatic experience and welcome it. This is not to say that Pentecostals have philosophically agreed with neo-orthodox views or consciously supported them. But Pentecostals have provided multitudes of people with thrilling experiences unrelated to intelligent doctrinal apprehension. 'Tongues' is the most prolific of these.

The new Testament from beginning to end demands that a believer receive an intelligible communication of objective truth if he is to be edified. (Compare 1 Cor. 14:1–19). Modern Pentecostals, however have spawned a 'tongues-speaking' which they claim edifies the speaker, but which they allow may be utterly unconnected with any apprehension of objective truth in the speaker. Here is the ideal existential experience of grace which cannot be verbally communicated to others in doctrine.[5]

It may be freely admitted that Pentecostals are too often correct in their criticism of Protestant churches for often having doctrine without life. The charge 'Dead Calvinism' has been made too often in denunciation of doctrinal churches to be altogether without foundation. Often a love for the truth is prone to degenerate into merely

[5] Sadly, David du Plessis appears completely unconscious of existential overtones in the meetings he attended with ecumenical leaders. He can even praise their evasion of truth as helpful to unity. See *The Spirit Bade Me Go*, p. 27.

intellectual exercises. Truth is philosophically enjoyed, while a longing for the Lord, a desire for holiness, love of the brethren, and determined obedience to the Lord's commands disappear. The human mind can follow the logic of pure doctrine and even assent to its correctness while the emotions are sterile and the will obstinate. Whole churches may be precise, yet lacking in deep worship, practical godliness and zeal for the Lord of Hosts.

Furthermore Pentecostals have diagnosed correctly the cause of this deplorable state of things. It is the absence of God's Spirit. Our Lord taught in John 6:63, 'It is the Spirit that quickeneth, the flesh profiteth nothing.' Human minds can be engaged in a reasoned study of lofty truths while wholly in the flesh. This accounts for young men who have taught the Scriptures faithfully but have never been born again. They can talk great doctrine to amaze even true believers. But true religion has never been set up in their hearts and their lives are worldly. Without the Spirit there may be intellectual understanding but there can be no experimental life. God's Word may be present, but without the Spirit it cannot be potent.

However, in reaction to Spiritless doctrine, Pentecostals have allowed a truthless spirit. Some neo-pentecostals openly spurn intellectual exercise as being contrary to the Spirit of God. And all

Pentecostals have allowed for the abstract intuitive communication of grace without the Word. An experience of tongues is said to be edifying to the subject who is altogether ignorant of the message or praise that his lips speak. It is claimed that the Spirit has brought experience and life in a devotional exercise of tongues where there is a vacuum so far as truth is concerned.

Scripture will no more admit the existence of life without the Word than it will without the Spirit. John 6:63 says, 'It is the Spirit that quickeneth; the flesh profiteth nothing: the words that I speak unto you, they are spirit, and they are life.' The life-giving work of the Spirit of God is so wed to the words of Christ that our Lord identifies His words and the Spirit. 'The words that I speak ... are spirit and they are life.' Christ is not referring to an abstract 'word' that may be encountered with intuitive blessing or to life-giving experience apart from intelligent communication. Rather it is *words* (plural) — actual vehicles of reasonable communication — that are used by the Spirit in bringing life to a soul.

Nowhere does the Bible allow a form of worship in which the reasoning faculties are suspended. 'God is a Spirit: and they that worship him must worship him in spirit and in truth' [John 4:24]. There can be no justification for calling any act of subjective emotionalism an act of worship prompted by the Spirit. Spirit and truth are always found together. The Spirit's workings are always attended with doctrinal content in the mind [1 Cor. 12:1–3] and self-control [1 Cor. 14:28–32].

If pentecostal leaders are fully serious about defending truth in their midst, then they will have to break their precious and fragile bonds of unity with the ignorant and deceived who come to them from churches largely apostate, and to speak out on truth. And they will have to come to abandon their own allowance of and encouragement of real edification apart from truth. Ultimately this can only lead them to an abandonment of their present dual system; on the one hand of demanding attention to Scripture to grow in grace, and on the other of holding out revelatory gifts and even 'ignorant tongues' as a means of edification. Only as Pentecostals are more and more removed from the main-stream of sensational gifts can their souls find adequate conditions for growth. When 'charismata' are laid aside the Bible can be taken up.

Believers who are curious or attracted to Pentecostalism are urged to heed a Biblical exhortation. When the apostle John commanded us to try the spirits, he did not suggest a subjective experiential test. He proposed an objective doctrinal measure for trying the spirits. 'Every spirit that confesseth that Jesus Christ is come in the flesh is of God' [1 John 4:2]. Confessions of faith, not reports of experience, are to hold our attention in testing spirits. All experience must be brought to the objective standard of the Word of God to be tested by its doctrines. It is not that Christians are against experience. But Spirit-given experience proceeds from an intelligent reception of the truth. It is not that Christianity is anti-emotional. The full range of human emotion is stirred by the Holy Ghost, but the Spirit stirs emotions by the truth.

When we look closely at the doctrines of the neo-pentecostal ranks, there is little to lead us to believe that the Spirit of truth is involved. There is much of excitement and spectacular experience. There is an explosion of emotional force. But there is pitifully little of mental exercise. There is almost no concern for doctrine. No teaching, no uniformity of dogma unites the modern 'charismatic' forces.

It is no wonder that expository preaching is so much absent from the excitement. Were the neo-pentecostals to begin to study the Bible in earnest they would discover that 'all scripture . . . is profitable for *doctrine*' [2 Timothy 3:16]. It would become clear that in order to save oneself and those that listen to him, one must 'take heed to doctrine' [1 Timothy 4:16]. Furthermore their members, by the blessing of the Spirit, would find Scripture sufficient as a means for meeting the Lord. They would no longer seek the hyper-experiences which Pentecostalism offers.

The great revival which is called the Reformation began with debates over doctrine. Serious study of the Word drove Luther, Calvin, Latimer and others to wrestle with doctrines such as Biblical authority, the bondage of the human will, justification by faith, the nature of the Lord's Supper, the nature of the church. The life of every true revival arose from attention given to truth. So it was in the days of our Lord. He was anointed with the Spirit to preach [Luke 4:18]. Each coming of the Spirit will produce doctrinal preaching. By truth the Spirit infuses life.

Any child of the truth must be distressed by the current neo-pentecostal movement. There truth is not springing out of the earth. It is being buried in a dreadful confusion. Blasphemy is sometimes welcomed. Biblical exposition is silenced in favour of spectacular testimonies of experience. Surely it is not too much to ask for true Christians that they pray on and wait on until God pours out his Spirit of holiness and truth. Surely genuine Christians are marked by a hunger for sound doctrine and a hunger for purity according to God's commandments.

There is no intention of suggesting that only pentecostal societies are found wanting in the essential tests of holiness and truth. All other branches of the 'evangelical world' share these woeful deficiencies. Precisely the same tests must be applied to any attractive fellowship. All spirits are to be tried, not only the pentecostal. They have been singled out in this chapter only because their distinctive doctrines are the main subject of our inquiry.

9: PERPLEXING
EXPERIENCE

Serious students of God's Word must deny that miracles are being performed today by men who are filled with God's Spirit. In the preceding pages we have argued that a scriptural examination of the general tone of the 'charismatic movement' leads to disappointment rather than to hope. The distinctive doctrine of all Pentecostals finds no Biblical support. Though numbers have been genuinely converted among neo-pentecostals, we cannot believe that revival is begun in this new 'protestant' force. Too much attention has been diverted from holiness and truth to happiness and experience. However, there may remain in the minds of some readers certain gnawing questions about the twentieth-century 'pentecostal' reports.

Is not their zeal in evangelism desirable? Does not 'full gospel' enthusiasm in missions prove that they have something to offer Christ's church today? Such questions are simply testing your real foundations. Are you thoroughly Biblical ? Or can 'success' and statistics draw you aside from a firm and exclusive devotion to the authority of Scripture?

'Jehovah's Witnesses' have a convincing zeal for their religion. Their missionary fervour puts many Christians to shame. Within their ranks many lives have been given new purpose and direction. But their errors are no less fatal. We are not implying that Pentecostals are so deeply entrenched in error as are 'Jehovah's Witnesses'. The comparison is intended only to illustrate that no doctrines or practices are to be imbibed because of impressive devotion to the winning of converts or to the degree of success attending such endeavours. Always we must ask, 'Do they speak according to God's Word?' 'If they speak not according to this word, it is because there is no light in them' [Isaiah 8:20].

Are we to think that neo-pentecostals are under some Satanic power? It must be admitted that, in any one instance, this is quite possible. Lying wonders of the wicked one continue to this day. Yet some who claim to have 'the gifts' are true servants of Christ with a genuine desire to know the Lord more fully. It is quite possible that their 'speaking in tongues' is an emotional or psychic phenomenon though unrecognized as such by the subject of the experience. There are others who have consciously induced similar speech experiences apart from being under the control of any spirit. But we must firmly deny that in either case men are prophesying! The Spirit of God has not given them inspired utterance.

'But', it may be asked, 'what of obvious healings

in neo-pentecostal meetings? Can you deny that God's power is at work?' If you are still asking this question, you are ignorant of much that is occurring today. Devoted enemies of the Scripture have held 'successful' healing meetings. Roman Catholics have claimed 'healing' by Mary at her shrines. Modernists have practised 'faith healing'. Their testimonies would be as difficult to refute as those of the Pentecostals. Yet we are certain that God's gracious power is not joined to their idols. How are we to explain these 'healings'? Are they psychosomatic ills removed by psychological means? Are they instances of the amazing power of mind over matter?[1].

It is possible to be certain that a work *is not* a miracle of man without being able to give a satisfactory explanation of what it *is*. At times the child of God must say, 'Though I have not the answer to all my questions, some things I do know.' We know that Jesus Christ is a sufficient prophet. His word is the only adequate authority for guiding our thoughts and actions. When Moses told God's redeemed people to have nothing to do with fortune-tellers, mystic counsellors and spiritual mediums of their day [Deuteronomy 18:9–12], it was not necessary to understand how

[1] We do not deny that God is healing men and women miraculously today in answer to the church's prayers. But *men* have not been given miraculous healing powers in our generation.

the spiritual quacks operated. It was not essential to be able to explain their effectiveness. It was only necessary to know that these things were an abomination to him and that they were to hearken to his prophet [Deuteronomy 18:12–15].

Knowing that God's Word to us is to come only from the Scriptures, and that miracles were performed only by men whose prophetic mission was to be confirmed, the Christian will be content to avoid the 'charismatic' ways of our generation. The unique and sufficient authority of the Bible is the foundation of all that we believe. Scrap God's Word for unexplainable events and soon the best doctrines will be lost. Allow spectacular experience to be your guide, and you will be blown about in very turbulent winds of doctrine which do not please God.

10: A POSITIVE WORD

It is a pity that one must be so negative as in former pages when handling the glorious work of the Holy Spirit. Yet one of the best methods for clarifying a truth is to contrast it with error. When darkness is the backdrop, light may be seen more clearly, provided that a preacher or writer does not content himself with condemning an error while failing to proclaim positive truth. Demolition work must prepare the way for a sturdy structure of truth.

One good that has come from neo-pentecostalism is a revived interest in the Holy Spirit. Pentecostals are quite right in saying that the church of Christ has neglected teaching about the Spirit. Their ability to lure men from the solid foundation of the apostles and prophets in the name of the Spirit proves their charge. The very demand for books such as this one indicts us for having slighted the third Person of the Trinity in teaching God's people.

Only as proper place in given in our churches to teaching concerning God the Spirit, will members be impregnable to errors touching his Person and work. Even were there no evils to guard against, it would be vital to instruct God's chosen people on the subject. Saints must be aware of the Spirit's glory in order to worship the Almighty in

a fully Biblical manner. They must understand
their utter dependence upon his work in receiving
the grace of God and in serving the living God.
Positive, mature appreciation of the Spirit and his
ministry will strengthen the church and will put
an end to radical searches for him which are
contrary to the Word.

Perhaps a few hints concerning the great
agency of the Spirit in the purposes of grace will
quicken a desire to know what the Scripture
teaches about him.[1] We need such knowledge,
not as an end in itself, but in order that the realization of our utter dependence upon him for
spiritual vitality may stir us up to pray more
urgently for the Spirit's presence.

As John the Baptist corrected his disciples' envy
toward Jesus, he testified of our Lord that 'God
giveth not the Spirit by measure unto him'
[John 3:34]. The incarnate Son of God did nothing in this world independent of God the Spirit.
Nothing in the glorious life of Christ can be
explained fully unless some attention is given to
the Spirit. If the Son of God was not to live upon
this earth without the constant ministry and
enablement of the Holy Ghost, it is not to be

[1] Many worthy volumes are in print, ready to guide your
study. John Owen *Works*, Vol. 3; *The Office and Work of
the Holy Spirit*, James Buchanan; and *The Work of the
Holy Spirit*, Octavius Winslow, are all available from The
Banner of Truth.

imagined that we mere creatures can please God in anything apart from the power of the Spirit.

It was by the Holy Spirit that the eternal Son was made flesh. He was 'conceived by the Holy Ghost'. Mary was stunned at the announcement that she would bear a son without intimately knowing a man. Gabriel explained, 'The Holy Ghost shall come upon thee, and the power of the Highest shall overshadow thee: therefore also that holy thing which shall be born of thee shall be called the Son of God' [Luke 1:35]. For the first time in history a holy thing (without the defilement of Adamic sin) was born of a woman. A divine act of the Spirit prepared a pure human nature for the Son of God.

Only the presence of the Spirit can explain the righteous life of Christ. Though the Son of God was eternally pure and spotless, in humbling himself to be made in the flesh he subjected himself to the ministry of the Spirit. The Spirit who brought Christ to a holy birth endowed him with positive grace to live in righteousness. Isaiah 11:1–5 ascribed the holiness of the Messiah to the immediate influence of the Spirit: 'The spirit of the Lord shall rest upon him, the spirit of wisdom and understanding, the spirit of counsel and might, the spirit of knowledge and of the fear of the Lord; and shall make him of quick understanding . . . And righteousness shall be the girdle of his loins, and faithfulness the girdle of his reins.' How did the incarnate Son maintain the fear of God in his heart while living with a cold, indifferent and obstinate human race? Where did the Saviour find the wisdom to escape every fierce temptation, the wisdom always to choose the good and refuse the evil? His sanctifying grace was from the Spirit!

By the same Holy Spirit our Lord carried out his mission for the Father. His entire course of obedience was bathed in the Spirit. To prepare him for his public ministry, the Spirit came upon Jesus at his baptism. All subsequent acts were performed in the power of the Spirit. 'And Jesus being full of the Holy Ghost returned from Jordan, and was led by the Spirit into the wilderness' [Luke 4:1]. 'And Jesus returned in the power of the Spirit into Galilee' [Luke 4:14]. Three years later at the cross on Calvary our Saviour 'through the eternal Spirit offered himself without spot to God' [Hebrews 9:14]. Afterward he was 'quickened by the Spirit' [I Peter 3:18], and raised to the right hand of the Father. Every part of Christ's redemptive work was accomplished with the divine assistance of the Holy Spirit.

Now, if the incarnate Son of God required the Spirit for his birth, holy living, and holy service to the Father, we too must always rely upon the Spirit's ministry. Apart from the Spirit of God there can be no rebirth in holiness for any man. The forming of holy character in the human soul is a work reserved for the sovereign Spirit. 'Except a man be born . . . of the Spirit, he cannot enter into the kingdom of God' [John 3:5]. He alone can quicken sinners to saving faith and repentance. Evangelism depends for its effectiveness upon the regenerating Spirit. Individual salvation comes only when this holy wind blows upon a man's heart.

As in the instance of Christ, all his disciples must have the Holy Ghost. Holiness blossoms and progresses in a life only when the Spirit gives his fruits. God's Word describes holy men as those who 'walk not after the flesh but after the Spirit' [Romans 8:1]. Service to our Lord is acceptable to him and efficient only when performed with the graces and gifts of his Spirit. Paul's apostolic exhortation must impress the soul: 'Be filled with the Spirit' [Ephesians 5:18].

How we need consciously to seek a greater portion of the Spirit's presence and blessing! We cannot condemn an interest in the third Person of the Trinity but heartily welcome it. Our Lord taught his disciples to pray for the Holy Spirit. In Luke 11:5–13 there is a parable illustrating the necessity for perseverance in prayer. That which our Lord envisages as being procured by persistent, fervent prayer is clearly disclosed when he promises that 'your heavenly Father (shall) give the Holy Spirit to them that ask him.'

Only by the Spirit will you be born 'a holy thing' in the image of Christ. Only by the Spirit can your loins be girded with holiness. Only by the Spirit can you present your body a living sacrifice, which is your reasonable service. Hence a great part of your prayer-work should be imploring the Almighty for a greater measure of his Spirit. It should be a daily exercise. Your Lord has taught you to ask for him!

Jesus received the Spirit without measure. Upon him came a fulness of the Spirit that no other man shall ever know. To him the Spirit gave the infinite perfection of every gift and grace. Nothing was held in reserve. The Spirit was granted in absolute fulness to God the Son. Others are anointed with the same Spirit, but he is 'anointed with the oil of gladness above his fellows' [Psalm 45:7].

In contrast with the Saviour, 'unto every one of us is given grace according to the measure of the gift of Christ' [Ephesians 4:7]. The Holy Spirit was perfectly given to the Son, who now is exalted at the Father's right hand of power and glory. Christ is the sovereign dispenser of the Spirit. He donates his gift to all his servants but in varying measures. With us there are higher and lower levels of sanctification, greater or lesser depth in worship, more or less ability and power in serving God. Always we can cry for more of the

Spirit – cry to him who has the Spirit immeasurably.

In earlier pages men were urged to cease their search for more of God's presence and blessings through a second work of grace. Scripture knows nothing of *one* experience subsequent to conversion which saints must pass through to enter a higher plane of spirituality. Especially the validity of Pentecostals' baptism with the Spirit and 'confirming' gifts was denied. All of this was *not* intended to advocate that you cease your quest for more of the Spirit's blessing. It was only intended to show that the second-work-of-grace teaching and Pentecostalism are bypaths to lead men off the road of following hard after God.

Paul prayed for the Ephesians: 'That he would grant you, according to the riches of his glory, to be strengthened with might by his Spirit in the inner man; that Christ may dwell in your hearts by faith; that ye, being rooted and grounded in love, may be able to comprehend with all saints what is the breadth, and length, and depth, and height; and to know the love of Christ, which passeth knowledge, that ye might be filled with all the fulness of God' [Eph. 3:16–19]. You must not count yourself to have apprehended, but you must ever press toward the mark of the high calling of God in Christ Jesus [Phil. 3:13 & 14]. To this end you daily need a strengthening with might by his

Spirit. Even if revival were to come by God's grace, you would not have apprehended, but would continue to require fresh grace. It is the goal set before you and your church, 'that ye might be filled with all the fulness of God.'

Oh that he would pour forth his Spirit of regeneration to quicken whole nations by his grace – to the praise of his infinite glory! Oh that he would grant a fuller measure of the Spirit of holiness to his church, that her purity might glisten and that she might appear beautiful on the earth! Oh that the mighty Monarch of our world would issue more of his Spirit of truth that understanding might deepen and proliferate through all the earth! Oh that the Spirit of worship would mightily humble assemblies before his face and draw us near to the holiest!

Pray for the Spirit. Pray for the Spirit who makes hearts love the doctrines of free and sovereign grace. Pray for the Spirit who expands hearts with a holy and reverent love for the Saviour. Pray for the Spirit who makes men ready for a battle against sin, patient in tribulation, zealous for the honour of God. The best remedy for excesses which dishonour the Spirit by using his name, is to live as a people filled with the Holy Spirit of truth and power. Pray for the Spirit of solid and Biblical revival!

11: THE HOLY SPIRIT
AND REVIVALS

Every true convert to Christ is baptized with the
Holy Ghost. All Christians form 'an holy temple
in the Lord', 'builded together for an habitation
of God through the Spirit' [Eph. 2:21 & 22].
Since Pentecost the blessed third Person of the
Trinity has taken up residence in the church of
Christ, never to depart from her, nor from any
true member of Christ's body. What a supreme
honour! What an extravagant privilege! Who can
comprehend the height of this dignity bestowed
on regenerate men? To be the very abode of the
living God Jehovah through the Spirit! It is the
cause of great wonder in us who so recently were
the vilest of sinners. A topic deserving of extended
joyful meditation and profuse thanksgiving!

In his worst moments, the child of God
remains baptized with the Holy Ghost. At her
lowest seasons, the true church is distinguished by
the indwelling presence of God the Holy Spirit.
At Pentecost a glorious donation was given the
Church on earth which shall never be withdrawn.
Because of the presence and consequent gracious
influences of the Spirit, 'he that is least in the
Kingdom of heaven is greater' than 'the stellar
John Baptist' [Matt. 11:11]. The Spirit is the
royal gift of our enthroned King all glorious

[Acts 2:33] and is thus the earnest of all our magnificent inheritance in him [Eph. 1:14].

Yet the gracious influences of the Spirit do not operate on the Christian or the church in an even flow of power and grace. It is possible for the indwelt church or believer to 'grieve the Holy Spirit of God' [Eph. 4:30]. Sin and indifference to truth are offensive to the holy Person dwelling within. Disregard for his inspired Word, together with worldly entanglements, may 'quench the Spirit' [I Thess. 5:19]. Believers may stifle, though true saints never will completely suppress, the Spirit's operations of grace on the heart. Sovereignly the Spirit chooses to intensify or decrease his influences in church and individual. There is an ebb and flow to the Spirit's power and fruits in the lives of individual Christians and in the history of the church. But never does the Spirit depart from the saint, and never is the church abandoned to herself.

There have been outstanding periods in the history of the church when the intensified activity of the Holy Spirit has amazed her. Such times are known as revivals. True revivals do not result from some special work of the Spirit of God different from his normal gracious influences! Rather they are the effect of an increased measure of precisely the same power and grace which operate at every time and in every place that the

[129]

church has been found since Pentecost. In revival times the Spirit's work remains what it has ever been since Pentecost, namely, the work of *inwardly* convincing the unconverted *by the Word*, *inwardly* regenerating sinners *by the Word*, *inwardly* teaching and sanctifying saints *by the Word*, and *inwardly* prompting worship of Father and Son *by the Word*.

What surprises in times of revival are not the operations of the Spirit but the accelerated pace with which he labours. His convincing and converting grace brings saving exercises upon the souls of great numbers instead of a few. Teaching and sanctifying influences are concentrated within a shorter span of time than is usually observed. Pastors are amazed at the firm grasp of Biblical truth in those who hear only a few sermons. Great strides are taken in practical godliness under the guidance of the Word. Worship and praise occupy entire communities. But it is nothing new or different. These things have always been done by the Spirit in Christ's church. In revival the work is intensified. The power and fruits of the Spirit come to flood tide. It is only with respect to the numbers affected, the speed of the process, and the intensity of the impressions that there is a difference. There is no difference in kind.

During past revivals there have arisen certain

trends in the thinking of the church and the
practice of believers which have paralleled the
posture of the modern pentecostal movement.
When these arose, the servants of God most
directly instrumental in the revivals have left the
much loved work of evangelism and teaching
vehemently to fight such trends. The stamping
out of attitudes like those central to today's
charismatic forces was considered more necessary
to the well-being of the church than the carrying
on with the revival. And when doctrines and
practices like those of 'full gospel' fame prevailed,
men most familiar with the experience of
revival noted that revivals were quenched by
them.

The Great Awakening by Joseph Tracy[1] is a
valuable volume on the revival connected with
the great names of Edwards, Whitefield, and the
Tennents. It quotes numerous first-hand reports
of the revival written by the pastors whose
preaching of truth was the chief human means of
revival. Their observations are of peculiar value
because they shepherded the revived flocks both
before and after the Great Awakening.

In all these reports, the ministers were careful
to deny that their labours in revival ministry had
any association whatever with revelations or miracles. With great joy many of them report in

[1] Tappan and Dennet, Boston (U.S.A.) 1842.

words such as these: 'We have not known trances, visions, revelations, or the like. We have had freedom from the appearances of a censorious spirit.'[2] This last report shows how revelations were classed with wicked shows of the flesh. Trances and visions did crop up, only to be crushed by responsible leaders.

New England pastors in revival fought every form of subjective guidance, even if this claimed to be of the Spirit. Their demand was that Scripture be the objective and the *only* guide to their practices. James Davenport for a time followed a subjective guidance and was considered a fanatic. Due to the labours of other pastors, he later renounced his former attitude in these words. 'I confess I have been much led astray by following impulses or impressions as a rule of conduct, whether they come with or without a text of Scripture; and my neglecting, also, duly to observe the analogy of Scripture. I am persuaded this was a great means of corrupting my experiences and carrying me off from the Word of God, and a great handle, which the false spirit has made use of with respect to a number, and me especially'.[3]

Aware that religious excitement could carry away multitudes, revival pastors laboured with

[2] Ibid. p. 127.
[3] Ibid. p 250.

unceasing zeal to examine every experience of converts by the doctrines of God's Word. Nothing was acceptable to them but the normal, inward operations of the Spirit in conviction, regeneration, and sanctification. Examinations were rigid. The following is typical of pastoral reports: 'They [the converts] can give a clear, distinct account of a preparatory law-work, in all the parts of it; of their discovery of Christ, in his ability, and willingness to save them in particular, and every way suited to their perishing circumstances, to make them completely and eternally happy; of their closing in with him as offered in the gospel; of the change of heart; and so consequently of principles, desires, inclinations and affections that perceptibly followed thereupon. And their lives and conversations, as far as I can observe myself, and learn from the unprejudiced, are corresponding and agreeing with their experiences.'[4]

Unusual outward manifestations attended the revivals. At times there were audible sighs and sobs throughout assemblies under the preached Word. Sometimes convicted sinners cried out, 'What must I do to be saved?', as Scripture was brought home to their consciences.[5] In a few instances men fell prostrate on the floor, even be-

[4] Ibid. p. 131
[5] Similar occurrences are recorded in the work carried on by David Brainerd among the Indians of N. America.

coming physically rigid for a time. What was the attitude of the pastors to these unusual happenings? All but a few 'fanatics' (as revival pastors called them) were completely unimpressed with these things. In speaking to the individuals who experienced them, they cared nothing for *outward* effects. They asked only what *inward* work had been done in their souls, and what truth of God's Word produced that *inward* experience. They were convinced that revival blessing was an inward and usual working of God's Holy Spirit by the Word of Scripture.

Congregations were urged to refrain from any public outburst or demonstration whatsoever so that none would be distracted from the truth. But pastors did not absolutely forbid these outward manifestations, for they found that truth had so mightily gripped the minds of some that they were overwhelmed. Again, it was an intelligent grasp of the inscripturated Word as a cause that led them to allow these phenomena. Let Tracy again be quoted: 'There have been not a very few among us within seven or eight months past, that have cried out with great agonies and distress, or with high joys on spiritual accounts, and that in time of religious exercises. But these two things we would observe relating to what we have seen of this nature, viz: First, that we are persuaded that very few, if any, among us, have cried out in such a manner while they could avoid it without doing too much violence to their nature, or turning their thoughts from divine things; though we have not thought it ordinarily proper to leave off speaking, or to have the persons so affected removed out of the house. And secondly, that *we by no means account* persons crying out in time of worship, falling down, or the degree of their joys or sorrows, that might occasion *these effects* on their bodies, *to be any sign of their conversion*, when separately considered; and have carefully warned our people against such a way of thinking; though at the same time we cannot but think that most who have so manifested their sense of things, were under the operations of the Holy Ghost at the same time, which occasioned these outcries; and that their inward experiences were substantially the same as theirs who have been savingly converted to God, as we hope, and have given no such tokens of their distress or joys.'[6]

Yet when outward effects became too great they hindered the work of revival. Jonathan Edwards says to this point: 'But when the people were raised to this height, Satan took the advantage, and his interposition in many instances soon became very apparent; and a great deal of caution and pains were found necessary to keep the people, many of them from running wild.'[7] Outward

[6] Ibid. pp. 126, 127.
[7] Ibid. p. 198.

excitement was not to be identified as the Spirit's work, nor was it a friend to revival.

Edwards notes among his people a trend of thinking about outward appearances which harmed them spiritually. He laboured long and hard against the attitude, as did many of his fellow pastors.[8] The regretted error was the conclusion that the height of *outward* extraordinary appearances was an index to the depth of *inward* spiritual experience. When they began to think that crying out was a sign of the Spirit's gracious influence, great damage was done. Their eyes became dazzled with the outward show. It took Edwards years of difficult endeavour to show that no outward excitement is proof of an inward spiritual experience.

That there are comparisons with modern Pentecostalism is obvious. Revelations other than God's Word are accepted and sought after. Its distinguishing doctrine is that an outward gift evidences inward grace. Pentecostalism fosters the very attitudes and opinions Edwards and others felt compelled to oppose if true revival was to continue. Pentecostalism is, today, the greatest friend of the idea that a man may be guided by impulse, and edified without a communication of objective truth from God's Word.

We are not now experiencing revival. Yet the

[8] Ibid. pp. 198–200.

great bulk of people in the church have been misled on the basic issues of truth, revelation and the indispensable necessity of Bible truth for experience in the Spirit. Pentecostalism is a major contributor to this regrettable state of affairs. If revivals ceased when men began to identify inward grace with an outward excitement; if revivals were hindered by reports of revelations; if revivals slackened when too much attention to the outward excitement drew attention from the objective truth of God's Word; then how can revivals begin when these conditions prevail in the church? Perhaps the destruction of the erroneous tenets of Pentecostalism is the most needed prelude to true revival. Any intensification of the Spirit's work would quickly run astray now, when few pastors can be found who will defend the absolute, unvarying necessity of the understanding of doctrine from God's Word if a soul is to receive a gracious work of his Spirit. Few will defend the *unique* authority and sufficiency of Scripture. How could a revival be kept on the only course in which the Spirit will work, that of the words of Christ? [John 6:63].

It is true that saints of past days referred to the outbreak of revival as 'pentecost'.[9] But the same men were horrified at the claims of others to

[9] Ibid. p. 142.

revelations and miracles.[10] Nor did they imagine that their revivals were anything but a larger supply of the same grace and power of the Spirit that they had always received in their churches. After revivals Christians were not in a category higher than those who never experienced them. It was no second work of grace. Nor was it a repetition of that unique historic occasion upon which the Spirit was newly given to the Church.

If these very men lived today, they would certainly disavow their own use of the term 'pentecost' to describe revival. In the context of our own times another designation would be found. They would draw back from the use of the word 'pentecost' lest anyone should imagine they had in mind the harmful doctrines of the 'charismatics'.

May the day quickly come when the doctrine of Scripture and its implications for experience are understood in the church, a day when it is firmly defended that the Spirit works *inwardly* upon the heart only in conjunction with an intelligent grasp of the *Words of Christ*! Then may the Spirit be pleased to employ his holy sword once more to accelerate, increase and intensify his *inward* conviction of the spirit *by the Word*. What a hope, to live at a time when the *inward* work of regeneration is wrought upon a

[10] Ibid. p. 148.

whole nation *by the Word*! It is worthy of our prayers that our understanding and inward graces be improved by an accelerated work of the Spirit through the means without which he will not work, namely, *the Word*. We shall never see another pentecost. But we may live to see greater fruits of the only historic Pentecost.

However, let us not be foolish children. Our hearts must not so pine for the Spirit's working by revival in this generation, that we invert our values. 'Ye have received the Spirit of adoption' [Rom. 8:15]. We are sons of Jehovah. God has put his Spirit in us. His glorious presence is not an earnest of revival but of the final glory and triumph of Christ. We shall be with him for evermore. The best of revivals pass away. But ours it is to be filled with all the fulness of God, to have him walk with us and dwell in us. Let us by the Spirit pray more for the return of Christ in great splendour, than we pray for revival! Then we shall be more Biblical. 'Even so, come, Lord Jesus.' [Rev. 22:20]. And meanwhile let us thank God for the Spirit and make him a welcome guest in our hearts.

APPENDIX:
THE TESTIMONY OF THE CHURCH[1]

The witness of so many leading preachers, theologians and commentators in the history of the church to the disappearance of the miraculous gifts of the apostolic age is a factor of considerable importance, especially as among them were men mightily used of the Spirit to awaken Continents to faith in Christ, men who in no way could be charged with grieving the Holy Spirit.

John Chrysostom (c347–407) writes in his commentary on spiritual gifts: 'This whole place is very obscure: but the obscurity is produced by our ignorance of the facts referred to and by their cessation, being such as then used to occur but now no longer take place' (*Homilies on First Corinthians*, Vol. XII, *The Nicene and Post-Nicene Fathers*, Hom. 29:2.).

Augustine (354–430) writes: 'In the earliest time the Holy Ghost fell upon them that believed: and they spake with tongues, which they had not learned, "as the Spirit gave them utterance." These were signs adapted to the time. For there behooved to be that betokening of the Holy Spirit

---

[1] The material from this Appendix has been supplied by my friend, Geoffrey Thomas, minister of the Baptist Church in Aberystwyth, Wales, to whom I am indebted.

in all tongues, and to shew that the Gospel of God was to run through all tongues over the whole earth. That thing was done for a betokening and it passed away.' ('Ten Homilies on the First Epistle of John', Vol. VII. *The Nicene and Post-Nicene Fathers*, VI, 10).

Thomas Watson writes in 1660: 'Sure, there is as much need of ordination now as in Christ's time and in the time of the apostles, there being then extraordinary gifts in the church which are now ceased' (*The Beatitudes*, 14).

John Owen writes in 1679: 'Gifts which in their own nature exceed the whole power of all our faculties, that dispensation of the Spirit is long since ceased and where it is now pretended unto by any, it may justly be suspected as an enthusiastic delusion' (*Works* IV, 518).

Matthew Henry writes on July 13, 1712: 'The gift of tongues was one new product of the spirit of prophecy and given for a particular reason, that, the Jewish pale being taken down, all nations might be brought into the church. These and other gifts of prophecy, being a sign, have long since ceased and been laid aside, and we have no encouragement to expect the revival of them; but, on the contrary, are directed to call the Scriptures the *more sure word of prophecy*, more sure than voices from heaven; and to them we are directed to *take heed*, to search them, and to hold them fast, 2 Peter 1:19' (Preface to Vol. IV of his *Exposition of OT & NT*, vii).

Jonathan Edwards writes in 1738 that the extraordinary gifts were given: 'in order to the founding and establishing of the Church in the world. But since the canon of the Scripture has been completed, and the Christian Church fully founded and established, these extraordinary gifts have ceased' (*Charity and its Fruits*, 29).

George Whitefield, because of his frequent testimony to the Person and power of the Spirit of God, was charged with 'enthusiasm' by some church leaders and was credited with believing that apostolic charismata were revived. This belief Whitefield firmly denied; 'I never did pretend to these extraordinary operations of working miracles, or speaking with tongues', ('Answer to the Bishop of London,' *Works* IV, 9). For failing to distinguish the ordinary and extra-ordinary work of the Spirit and for considering *both* to have ceased he blames the Bishop and clergy of Lichfield and Coventry, 'who reckon the indwelling, and inward witnessing of, as also praying and preaching by the Spirit, among the *karismata*, the miraculous gifts conferred on the primitive church, and which have long since ceased.' ('Second letter to the Bishop of London', *Works*, Vol. IV, 167). Whitefield's friends also defended him from the same false charge. Joseph

Smith, for example, Congregational pastor in South Carolina, wrote of the English evangelist: 'He renounced all pretences to the extraordinary powers and signs of apostleship, peculiar to the age of inspiration, and extinct with them.' (In Preface to *Sermons on Important Subjects*, George Whitefield, 1825, xxv).

James Buchanan writes in 1843: 'The miraculous gifts of the Spirit have long since been withdrawn. They were used for a temporary purpose. They were the scaffolding which God employed for the erection of a spiritual temple. When it was no longer needed the scaffolding was taken down, but the temple still stands, and is occupied by his indwelling Spirit; for, "Know ye not that ye are the temple of God, and that the Spirit of God dwelleth in you" (1 Cor. 3:16).' (*The Office and Work of the Holy Spirit*, 34).

Charles Haddon Spurgeon in a number of sermons testifies to this same view. The apostles, he preached, were 'men who were selected as witnesses because they had personally seen the Saviour – an office which necessarily dies out, and properly so, because the miraculous power also is withdrawn' (*Met. Tab. Pulpit* 1871, Vol. 17, 178). And again, 'Although we may not expect and need not desire the miracles which came with the gift of the Holy Spirit, so far as they were physical, yet we may both desire and expect that which was intended and symbolized by them, and we may reckon to see the like spiritual wonders performed among us at this day' (*Met. Tab. Pulpit* 1881, Vol. 27, 521). Again, 'those works of the Holy Spirit which are at this time vouchsafed to the Church of God are every way as valuable as those earlier miraculous gifts which have departed from us. The work of the Holy Spirit, by which men are quickened from their death in sin, is not inferior to the power which made men speak with tongues' (*Met. Tab. Pulpit.* 1884, Vol. 30, 386 ff.).

Robert L. Dabney, writes in 1876, that after the early Church had been established: 'the same necessity for supernatural "signs" now no longer existed, and God, who is never wasteful in his expedients, withdrew them. Henceforward, the Church was to conquer the belief of the world by its example and teachings alone, energized by the illumination of the Holy Spirit. Finally, miracles, if they became ordinary, would cease to be miracles, and would be referred by men to customary law' ('Prelacy a Blunder', *Discussions: Evangelical and Theological*, Vol. 2, 236–237).

George Smeaton writes in 1882: 'The supernatural or extraordinary gifts were temporary, and intended to disappear when the Church should be founded and the inspired canon of Scripture closed; for they were an external proof of an internal inspiration' (*The Doctrine of the Holy Spirit*, 51).

Abraham Kuyper writes in 1888: 'Many of the charismata, given to the apostolic church, are not of service to the church of the present day' (*The Work of the Holy Spirit*, 182, Eng. ed. 1900).

W. G. T. Shedd writes also in 1888: 'The supernatural gifts of inspiration and miracles which the apostles possessed were not continued to their ministerial successors, because they were no longer necessary. All the doctrines of Christianity had been revealed to the apostles, and had been delivered to the church in a written form. There was no further need of an infallible inspiration. And the credentials and authority given to the first preachers of Christianity in miraculous acts, did not need continual repetition from age to age. One age of miracles well authenticated is sufficient to establish the divine origin of the gospel. In a human court, an indefinite series of witnesses is not required. "By the mouth of two or three witnesses," the facts are established. The case once decided is not reopened.' (*Dogmatic Theology*, Vol. II, 369).

Benjamin B. Warfield writes in 1918 'These gifts were not the possession of the primitive Christian as such; nor for that matter of the Apostolic Church or the Apostolic age for themselves; they were distinctively the authentication of the Apostles. They were part of the credentials of the Apostles as the authoritative agents of God in founding the church. Their function thus confined them to distinctively the Apostolic Church and they necessarily passed away with it' (*Counterfeit Miracles*, 6).

Arthur W. Pink writes in a book which appeared in 1970: 'As there were offices extraordinary (apostles and prophets) at the beginning of our dispensation, so there were *gifts* extraordinary; and as successors were not appointed for the former, so a continuance was never intended for the latter. The gifts were *dependent upon the offices*. We no longer have the apostles with us and therefore the supernatural gifts (the communication of which was an essential part of "the signs of an apostle", II Cor. 12:12) are absent' (*The Holy Spirit*, 179).

SELECT BIBLIOGRAPHY

(Titles published by The Banner of Truth Trust,
unless otherwise indicated)

James Buchanan, *The Office and Work of the
Holy Spirit*

Frederick D. Bruner, *A Theology of the Holy
Spirit* [Eerdmans and Hodders]

Jonathan Edwards, *A Narrative of Surprising
Conversions; Charity and its Fruits*

John Owen, *A Discourse Concerning the Holy
Spirit etc; Works*, Vols. 3 and 4

J. C. Ryle, *Holiness* [James Clarke]

George Smeaton, *The Doctrine of the Holy
Spirit*

Richard C. Trench, *Notes on the Miracles of our
Lord* [Macmillan].

Rowland S. Ward, *Spiritual Gifts in the Apostolic
Church*. [Private publication].

B. B. Warfield, *Counterfeit Miracles*

Octavius Winslow, *The Work of the Holy Spirit*